# Introduction

The new National Curriculum for 2014 places particular pressures on subject leaders in primary and secondary schools in maintaining high quality teaching, effective use of resources and improved standards at a time of curriculum change.

Scholastic Education, publisher of the bestselling 100 Lessons series, has partnered with Babcock Learning and Development Partnership, one of the UK's leading school improvement services, to develop these essential subject guides, which can be used to support your colleagues in understanding and responding to the curriculum changes.

For the first time, the Department for Education has made the new National Curriculum for 2014 available in digital format only. We understand that a printed copy of the Curriculum is a useful tool in communicating these changes and as such a complete printed programme of study for Mathematics Key Stages 1-3 has been included in each Subject Leader's Guide.

Each Guide also offers:

- Explanation of the changes to the English curriculum and the subject leader's role in implementing these changes
- Advice on the content and expectations of the curriculum, and priority areas for each key stage (KS1-3)
- Support for structuring the curriculum including advice on lesson planning and guidance for developing a calculations policy
- Information on OfSted's expectations and role in inspecting maths teaching in your school.

Finally, we offer a useful checklist for any maths subject leader to follow in moving towards the new curriculum.

We hope this Subject Leader's Guide proves to be a useful tool and wish you every success in implementing the new curriculum in your school.

Scholastic Education

Babcock LDP

# Changes to the mathematics National Curriculum

## Attainment targets

The previous National Curriculum had four attainment targets with level descriptors. In the 2014 National Curriculum there is one overarching attainment target and no level descriptors with new performance descriptors to be introduced to inform statutory teacher assessment:

*By the end of each key stage, pupils are expected to know, apply and understand the matters, skills and processes specified in the relevant Programme of Study.*

## Programmes of Study

The Programmes of Study in the previous National Curriculum were set out for each key stage. In the 2014 National Curriculum they have been set out on a yearly basis for Key Stages 1 and 2, although the curriculum is only statutory at the key-stage level (see below). The 2014 Mathematics Programmes of Study for Key Stages 1, 2 and 3 are arranged in Domains such as, addition and subtraction, fractions, measurement and so on.

The Domains are a convenient way of organising the curriculum on paper. However, it is made clear in the aims that the intention is that these are NOT taught separately but rather that conceptual links are made:

*Mathematics is an interconnected subject in which pupils need to be able to move fluently between representations of mathematical ideas. The Programmes of Study are, by necessity, organised into apparently distinct Domains, but pupils should make rich connections across mathematical ideas to develop fluency, mathematical reasoning and competence in solving increasingly sophisticated problems.*

Making connections is at the heart of mathematics and teaching should make explicit connections between Domains. For example, the KS1 number and place value objective, *compare and order numbers from 0 up to 100*, should be taught with the measurement objective, *compare and order lengths, mass, volume/capacity*. Similarly, at KS3 there are clear links with, for example, fractions and percentages appearing both in the number and ratio, proportion and rates of change Domains.

## Using and applying

There is no Programme of Study for 'Using and applying mathematics' and therefore no progression. It is instead encapsulated in the aims at the front of the maths National Curriculum. These aims are of vital importance to the whole curriculum; it is intended that they are part of all mathematics in schools and understanding the intention and scope of the aims will be an important aspect of creating a curriculum which develops pupils as mathematical thinkers. Thinking is at the heart of mathematics and should be at the heart of mathematical teaching and learning.

*The National Curriculum for mathematics aims to ensure that all pupils:*

- *become **fluent** in the fundamentals of mathematics, including through varied and frequent practice with increasingly complex problems over time, so that pupils develop conceptual understanding and the ability to recall and apply knowledge rapidly and accurately.*

**SCHOLASTIC**

The use of the term 'fluent' needs to be fully understood. It is important to notice that conceptual understanding is included as part of fluency, which moves it beyond simple memorisation of facts and procedures and requires that pupils are making decisions. Russell (2000) suggests that fluency is possible only when you have:

- *an understanding of the meaning of the operations and their relationships to each other – for example, the inverse relationship between multiplication and division*
- *the knowledge of a large repertoire of number relationships, including the addition and multiplication facts as well as other relationships, such as how 4 × 5 is related to 4 × 50*
- *a thorough understanding of the base ten number system, how numbers are structured in this system, and how the place value system of numbers behaves in different operations – for example, that 24 + 10 = 34 or 24 × 10 = 240.*

This means that teachers need to focus on building conceptual understanding and making explicit connections so that pupils make decisions, using what they know and understand, to solve problems.

*The National Curriculum for mathematics aims to ensure that all pupils:*

- **reason mathematically** *by following a line of enquiry, conjecturing relationships and generalisations, and developing an argument, justification or proof using mathematical language.*

Pupils need to get underneath what is going on and understand the structures underpinning the mathematics so that they can generalise and use and apply their understanding. This expectation means that teachers need to focus their teaching on the structure of the mathematics they are engaged with rather than how 'to do' the maths. Contrast a KS2/KS3 lesson in which the objective is for pupils to 'know how to solve an equation' with one in which they learn about equations.

For this aim to be fully realised, teachers need to consider what it is they want pupils to think, notice and understand about the structure of the mathematics while they are engaged in activities, and therefore what it is they want the pupils to be able to generalise.

This aim also requires that pupils communicate their mathematical thinking and respond to other people's thinking, making talk for maths a key part of learning mathematics. Talk in maths classrooms needs to involve rich dialogue which is underpinned by an expectation that everyone takes responsibility for making themselves understood and pupils aim to make sense of what everyone else says.

*The National Curriculum for mathematics aims to ensure that all pupils:*

- *can* **solve problems** *by applying their mathematics to a variety of routine and non-routine problems with increasing sophistication, including breaking down problems into a series of simpler steps and persevering in seeking solutions.*

The expectation in this aim is that pupils will be engaging with problems which challenge their thinking; the inclusion of perseverance indicates that this aim goes beyond simple word problems. In *Mathematics: Made to Measure* (Ofsted 2012), the issue of a reliance on word problems in primary schools was identified:

*In the primary schools, opportunities to use and apply mathematics were generally restricted to solving 'word problems'. Typically pupils were given sets of word problems, all of which required the same recently learnt operation or method, for example several problems all solved by using subtraction. Such practice does not promote good problem-solving skills because pupils do not have to think the approaches through for themselves.*

Problem solving should involve the pupils in:

- *seeking solutions not just memorising procedures*
- *exploring patterns not just memorising formulas*
- *formulating conjectures, not just doing exercises.* (Pólya 1945)

It needs to be understood at a whole-school level that working mathematically involves being stuck, redrafting and trying different approaches to solve a problem. Mathematicians do not look at a problem that is worthwhile and immediately know the correct route through it.

The aims of the National Curriculum indicate the intention that using and applying is at the heart of mathematics teaching and learning. The danger of the way the new primary curriculum is presented is that these core aims are at the front of the document only; because they don't appear in each year group, it is possible that they will be missed by some teachers. In shaping the curriculum in their schools, subject leaders need to ensure that all teachers have an understanding of the aims and that they underpin mathematics throughout the school.

## Content and expectations

The 2014 National Curriculum does include some increase in expectations: KS1 contains content that previously was identified as Level 3 and sat within KS2, and KS2 now includes elements that were previously part of the KS3 curriculum. Changes include:

- **Number and place value**: Higher expectations in counting in KS1 (now includes counting in threes) and in KS2 the inclusion of Roman numerals linked to an understanding of how our current number system has developed over time, with experience of Roman numerals providing a context for understanding place value. The language of number is also clarified with 'ones' being used in place of 'units' throughout.
- **Addition and subtraction**: KS1 includes mentally adding and subtracting pairs of two-digit numbers; this was previously in KS2 and underpins what follows in the new KS2 curriculum. The notion of 'levels of accuracy' is introduced in KS2 and the use of calculators has been removed from KS2 (see below under multiplication and division).
- **Multiplication and division**: This includes recall of multiplication facts up to 12 × 12 (previously it was 10 × 10) in KS2. The understanding of composite numbers has been included in KS2 and there is specific reference to solving scaling and correspondence problems. There are also detailed expectations around the use of short and long multiplication and division, and the use of calculators has been removed from KS2. The expectation is that calculators will still be used in primary schools (see the introduction to Mathematics at KS1–2 under 'ICT') but the removal of calculators from the Programmes of Study in KS2 suggests that some pupils may need to be taught the appropriate use of a calculator at KS3.

**SCHOLASTIC**

- **Fractions (including decimals and percentages)**: Generally there are earlier and more challenging expectations for fractions and decimals. Fractions in the KS1 curriculum was previously about introducing halves and quarters; the 2014 Curriculum includes understanding of $\frac{1}{2}$, $\frac{1}{3}$, $\frac{1}{4}$, $\frac{2}{4}$ and $\frac{3}{4}$ in KS1, including equivalence of $\frac{1}{2}$ and $\frac{2}{4}$. Fractions in KS2 includes: adding, subtracting, multiplying and dividing fractions.

- **Measurement**: There are increased expectations around the use of standard units in KS1 and in relation to telling the time. In KS2, area was previously limited to rectangles and shapes composed of rectangles but now includes parallelograms and triangles and the use of formulae to calculate the area of different shapes. Volume has been moved into KS2, including the use of formulae to calculate volume.

- **Geometry – properties of shapes**: The expectations in KS2 include knowing about the angles in any regular polygon, illustrating and naming parts of circles (including knowing the relationship between the diameter and radius and expressing this algebraically) and finding missing angles, including those on a straight line and vertically opposite angles, all of which was previously in KS3. At KS3 the expectations include the use of trigonometric ratios to solve problems involving right-angled triangles.

- **Geometry – position and direction**: In KS1 the increased expectation around fractions is reflected in relation to turning where three-quarter turns are included. In KS2 the expectations include reflecting shapes in the axes of a coordinate grid (all four quadrants).

- **Statistics**: Previously there was no handling data in KS1; statistics is included in KS1 in the 2014 Curriculum and involves interpreting and constructing pictograms, tally charts, block diagrams and simple tables and answering questions about the data by counting, adding and subtracting. In KS2 interpreting and constructing pie charts has been introduced along with calculating the mean as an average. Mode and probability have been removed from KS2. This means that the first time that pupils will meet probability is at KS3 where probability and statistics are two distinct Domains. The probability Domain states that pupils should be taught to *enumerate sets and unions/intersections of sets systematically, using tables, grids and Venn diagrams*. In the statistics Domain at KS3 the use of vertical line charts is included.

- **Ratio and proportion**: There is generally an increased requirement for understanding proportional reasoning that is reflected in the expectations for multiplication and division and fractions. In this specific Domain in KS2 there is an explicit link made between percentages and constructing pie charts and solving problems involving similar shapes where the scale factor is known or can be found. The inclusion of a ratio and proportion Domain in KS3 is one of the more significant changes at this level with this Domain placing much greater emphasis on proportional reasoning, linking fractions, ratio and percentages as different representations of multiplicative relationships.

- **Algebra**: The expectation in KS2 is that algebra will be used in all areas of the maths curriculum, for example in measuring area and volume and calculating the angles of a triangle. This depends on the foundations being laid in KS1 and throughout KS2 even though there is no Programme of Study for algebra in KS1. Drawing a distinction between algebra and algebraic notation may open further opportunities for development of algebra through all keys stages. Working and thinking algebraically at KS1 and KS2 will support the more rigorous requirements for formal algebraic notation at KS3.

# Priority areas for engaging with the mathematics National Curriculum

## Understanding the statutory requirements

It is important for schools to understand that although the curriculum is set out on a yearly basis for Years 1 to 6, it is only statutory at the key-stage level.

*The Programmes of Study for mathematics are set out year-by-year for Key Stages 1 and 2.* **Schools are, however, only required to teach the relevant programme of study by the end of the key stage. Within each key stage, schools therefore have the flexibility to introduce content earlier or later than set out in the programme of study.**

This gives rise to a significant opportunity and a potential threat:

### Opportunity to shape the curriculum

A curriculum which is statutory at the key-stage level allows schools the freedom to shape their curriculum and requires teachers to make important decisions about its structure. It provides the opportunity for teachers to be creative designers of learning, rather than deliverers of a prescribed curriculum, and this should start from agreed values, aims and principles which underpin the teaching and learning of maths in a school, and have a direct impact on curriculum planning.

For the mathematics curriculum, an important part of the process will be agreeing a progression in calculation through a calculation policy (see below).

Designing the mathematics curriculum at each key stage will also need to take into account the fact that what is listed in the National Curriculum is just one element in the education of every pupil and that:

*Teachers should develop pupils' numeracy and mathematical reasoning in all subjects so that they understand and appreciate the importance of mathematics.*

This means that the designing of the curriculum should include identifying cross-curricular links and creating opportunities for rich mathematical experiences across the curriculum. At KS3 the organisational structure of a secondary context is likely to make this more challenging. Work will need to be done across the school with different departments to create a dialogue. This should be a two-way process asking *What are the mathematics requirements for each department?* (these may be very precise – for example, a PE department may need to know how to calculate 70% of a maximum heart rate), as well as raising awareness of calculation strategies used by pupils and the importance of mathematical thinking and reasoning. It is possible that many departments will think that there is no mathematics in their subject but, by supporting them to broaden their understanding of what mathematics is (not just number work), opportunities are likely to become more apparent.

*All schools are also required to set out their school curriculum for mathematics on a year-by-year basis and make this information available online.*

The fact that the curriculum is statutory at the key-stage level may be masked for teachers by the way that the Programmes of Study for mathematics are set out year-by-year for KS1–2. This provides a potential threat; teachers cannot rely on following the curriculum in one year group but may think that they can. Instead, they need to understand the expectations across the whole key stage and the previous key stage.

This is partly because it is assumed that the areas of maths included in one year group continue to be developed in the following year groups without necessarily being explicitly mentioned. One example of this is the teaching of coordinates in KS2. The key stage expectation is that pupils will be able to work with coordinates in the four quadrants. However, in the year-by-year setting out of the Programmes of Study, coordinates in the first quadrant are introduced in Year 4, there is no mention of them in the Year 5 Programme of Study and then coordinates in four quadrants are included in the Year 6 Programme of Study. A Year 5 teacher looking only at the Year 5 Programmes of Study may think that this is not an area they need to cover but the expectation is that this is an area of understanding which is developed in KS2, not only in Year 4 and Year 6.

The importance of looking across key stages is exemplified by the fact that in Year 3 there is no mention of adding and subtracting pairs of two-digit numbers mentally because this appears in Year 2; children should still be making decisions about when to do this when solving problems and developing and using this skill further in KS2.

## Planning a route through the curriculum

To design a curriculum that has making connections at its heart, it will be necessary to plan a route that brings together the learning from the different Domains, in a meaningful way. One way to achieve this is to structure the learning around key themes that build on each other and bring together related aspects of mathematics. These themes in KS1 and KS2 could be:

- **Number sense**: This theme is about understanding our number system, starting with counting numbers and building on this to include negative numbers, fractions and decimals. The focus is on building an understanding of how our numbers work and fit together and includes exploring place value, comparing and ordering numbers and rounding, and applying this understanding in different contexts. Understanding the number system underpins calculation and running a teaching sequence on number sense prior to a calculation sequence would support pupils to make links.

- **Additive reasoning**: This theme is about understanding addition and subtraction together and the relationship between them, using this understanding to solve problems in different contexts, including measures and statistics. The expectation is that pupils of all ages appropriately choose and use number facts, understanding of place value and different methods starting with counting and mental methods and developing into mental and written methods, explaining their decision making and justifying their solutions.

- **Multiplicative reasoning**: This theme is about understanding multiplication and division together and the relationship between them, clearly connecting to this an understanding of fractions both as operators, for example the equivalence between dividing by five and multiplying by a fifth, and the outcome of divisions, for example understanding $3 \div 4 = {}^3/_4$. This understanding is used to solve problems in different contexts, including measures and statistics. The expectation is that pupils of all ages appropriately choose and use number facts, understanding of place value and different methods starting with counting and mental methods and developing into mental and written methods, explaining their decision making and justifying their solutions.

- **Geometric reasoning**: This theme is about understanding properties of shapes and the relationship between them, using this understanding to solve problems including problems related to measures (perimeter, area and volume), and understanding movement within space. The expectation is that pupils of all ages appropriately choose and use facts and understanding, explaining their decision making and justifying their solutions.

(These themes form the basis of a planning framework written by Babcock LDP in 2013.)

At KS3 some of these themes may not be appropriate while some may need to be explored in greater breadth and depth. Additional themes may also need to be included. For example, you might like to consider:

- **Algebraic reasoning**: This theme is about both algebraic notation and algebraic thinking. The focus is on understanding relationships and structures, and communicating these through the convention of algebraic notation. The expectation is that pupils are able to use notation to model a problem or situation, or to describe a reason or structure eventually leading to simple proofs.

- **Reasoning about data and uncertainty**: This theme brings together the Domains of statistics and probability, using mathematics to consider and reason about risk, explore the validity of arguments and to make good decisions. The expectation is that pupils understand how mathematics and statistics are used and misused to represent data, and are able to interpret and draw their own conclusions given appropriate evidence, and to know how to find evidence if none is available.

## Planning teaching sequences and lessons

Once a route through the curriculum has been established, medium-term planning of teaching sequences will be necessary. These sequences will make clear connections between areas of mathematics, encouraging pupils to use what they know and understand rather than treating each area of maths as separate and unconnected. The teaching sequences should have a clear destination (success criteria) with teachers planning the journey, identifying the places it must pass (linked to objectives from the Programmes of Study) to reach the destination. Teaching sequences might run over two or three weeks and detailed lesson planning will only be possible up to a few days in advance as assessment for learning should feed into and influence the planning.

When planning lessons, teachers are looking to support pupils to make cognitive connections. One model for teaching and learning mathematics that can support planning for this focus on connections is shown below.

◨SCHOLASTIC

It connects different representations of a mathematical concept: contexts, language, mathematical images/pictures and symbols.

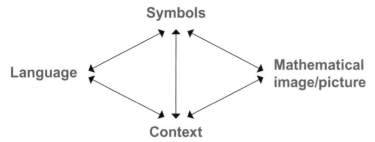

(Adapted by the Babcock LDP Primary Maths Team from by Haylock and Cockburn 1989)

For example:

- A class might be looking at how to reduce their school's impact on the environment and decide to focus on how the pupils travel to school. This provides the context and purpose for the mathematics.

- The pupils examine the data that has been collected, which shows the number of pupils who walk, cycle or travel by car, bus or taxi, and talk about what they notice and what they would like to change; this will involve both mathematical and contextual language, being used as part of purposeful talk.

- A question arises about the total number of pupils who travel in a vehicle that uses fuel compared to the number of pupils who travel in a sustainable way. This provides an opportunity for the pupils to look at the most efficient way to add the numbers, using what they know and understand.

- A mathematical image might be used to support understanding of a method; for example, understanding that for 165 + 25 it is easy to partition the second number and use the known facts 5 + 5 = 10 and 7 + 2 = 9 (for 70 + 20 = 90). The image might also be used by a pupil to support their explanation of their method, allowing others to access their thinking.

- Images for addition include base ten, number lines, bead strings and place-value counters and the focus should be on using the image to support understanding, not 'to do' the maths. Counting in ones should be avoided and decisions about which images to have available should depend on them being fit for purpose and decisions about which to use to support explanations should be made by the pupils. The symbols might record the steps taken or the calculation undertaken (165 + 5 + 20 = 190 or 165 + 25 = 190) and the pupils should be able to explain the symbols in relation to the maths of the context, which will involve revisiting relevant language.

As pupils develop their skills, the scaffolding should be reduced. Imagine a hypothetical learning walk in which you are able to visit a classroom of Year 1 pupils, then Year 2, then Year 3 and so on up to the end of KS3. Not only would you expect the content of the lessons to be increasingly challenging, you should also expect the way in which pupils experience this content to be more demanding, with pupils building problem-solving skills alongside developing fluency with and conceptual understanding of the mathematical content being worked on. When planning, consideration needs to be given to what content is to be taught and also how that content is to be experienced.

# Developing a calculation policy

*A feature of strong practice in the maintained schools is their clear, coherent calculation policies and guidance, which are tailored to the particular school's context. They ensure consistent approaches and use of visual images and models that secure progression in pupils' skills and knowledge lesson by lesson and year-by-year.*

*(Good Practice in Primary Mathematics: Evidence From 20 Successful Schools Ofsted 2011)*

Calculation is a significant part of the maths curriculum and it will be necessary for schools to review their calculation policy or create a new one in light of the 2014 Curriculum. It is also important that the policy goes beyond the content of the 2014 Curriculum because:

- There is limited detail for mental calculation. A calculation policy should set out progression in mental calculation and make explicit that mental calculation will be part of calculation at all stages.

- The structures of the operations are not set out clearly; some appear in the statutory Programmes of Study, some in the non-statutory guidance and some don't appear at all. The calculation policy should include: understanding addition as combining (aggregation) and counting on (augmentation); understanding subtraction as taking away, finding the difference between and 'how many more to make' (complementary addition); understanding multiplication as repeated addition and scaling; and understanding division as equal sharing and grouping. Both multiplication and division should include understanding correspondence problems.

- Expectations in relation to language are not clearly laid out. As well as the range of mathematical vocabulary, this should include related contextual language and structuring mathematical sentences related to calculation in different contexts. Structuring sentences can be a challenge when the language does not appear in the same order as the symbols but it is vital that pupils can match different situations to the same symbols, for example 'Three fewer than seven is four' and 'Seven minus three equals four' are matched to $7 - 3 = 4$.

- Representation appears in some places but there is no detail of what to use where and why. Mathematical images can be used to support understanding of calculation at all stages but the images that are most appropriate will vary according to the mathematics and the needs of the pupils. Images are best used to expose structure and make connections explicit; they should not be relied on for 'doing' the maths, which often results in counting in ones, apart from at the earliest stage.

- Decision making does not feature strongly in the Programmes of Study and yet this underpins fluency and needs to be highlighted within any calculation policy. All calculation should involve decision making with pupils expected to choose and use appropriate methods; this allows teachers to assess understanding of calculation. Pupils at all stages should be expected to make, explain and justify decisions. Linked to decision making are efficiency, checking and estimating and these also need to be part of the calculation policy.

Primary schools might consider working with other schools in their area, including secondary schools, to develop a common core to their calculation policies, or a common policy, ensuring that there is continuity for pupils as they transfer into KS3.

# The subject leader's role in preparing for the new curriculum

## Overview

The primary mathematics subject leader has a key role to play in preparing staff for the new curriculum. Auditing against the priority areas above will allow them to develop an overview of the needs in the school and draw up a strategic plan. Auditing may include: talking with pupils, learning walks, observations of teaching, talking with staff, work scrutiny, reviewing planning and data analysis.

One approach is to start with what you are already doing well and clearly identify areas for development as follows:

- Evaluate attainment and progress – information gathered from data analysis and talking with pupils.
    - How well are pupils doing in relation to national standards?
    - Are pupils making good or better progress?
    - Are there differences in attainment or progress across the school? Groups of pupils such as FSM/boys/girls? Key stages or classes?
- Identify pedagogical approaches that are effective – information gathered from talking with pupils, learning walk, observation of teaching, work scrutiny, reviewing planning.
    - How do we teach this area currently?
    - Is the teaching approach consistent across the school?
    - Are there areas of significant expertise or weakness?
    - How do staff feel about teaching in this area?
    - How do pupils feel about their learning in this area?
- Identify staff subject knowledge strengths and areas for development – information gathered from observation of teaching, talking to staff.
    - Do staff feel confident to deliver expectations of new curriculum?
    - Is there evidence that they are confident with subject knowledge?
- Consider the needs of your school community – information gathered talking to pupils, talking to staff, reviewing planning.
    - How well does the maths curriculum reflect your location and the needs of the pupils?
    - Are pupil's interests met through the maths curriculum?

Further guidance on talking to pupils can be found at the Babcock LDP website in Primary Maths Paper 4 and details from Ofsted about work scrutiny and observation are in the section on Ofsted below.

### Continuing professional development

Once a subject leader has identified the development needs of staff around the teaching and learning of the new maths curriculum, decisions need to be made about the type of support that will be provided. The Centre for the Use of Research and Evidence in Education (CUREE) reviewed research to identify characteristics of effective CPD which has an impact on pupils and summarised these as:

- *Sustained collaboration with professional colleagues, including both making use of specialist expertise and structured peer support for embedding specialist contributions.*

- *An understanding of and commitment to professional learning, including enquiry-oriented learning and learning to learn from looking.*
- *A focus on refining teaching and learning, working towards aspirations for specific pupils side by side with theory.*
- *Effective scaffolding and modelling of learning by both teachers and leaders for colleagues and for pupils.*

(Philippa Cordingley 2013)

In addition to this, research by Robinson *et al* (2009) found that a key factor in the success of CPD is the involvement of head teachers.

*Of all the activities…head teachers' leading of and active participation in professional learning and development had the largest impact on student outcomes. Their involvement could be in:*

- *formal contexts such as staff meetings and professional development sessions, and*
- *informal contexts such as discussions about specific teaching problems.*

### Supporting teaching and planning

Subject leaders can support staff with identifying rich activities which fit with the aims of the National Curriculum, supporting pupils with making connections and involve reasoning. Collections of such activities can be found on the Nrich website and the National STEM Centre has archived many useful materials, including investigations collected together by Gillian Hatch and National Strategy ITPs and Excel Spreadsheets, within its elibrary. The National Centre for the Excellence in Teaching Mathematics (NCETM) has been funded to bring together resources to support teaching and CPD in relation to the new curriculum.

### Ofsted

Key documents published by Ofsted indicate expectations about teaching and learning maths in primary schools: *Good Practice in Primary Mathematics: Evidence From 20 Successful Schools* (2011); *Mathematics: Made to Measure* (2012); and *Mathematics Subject Survey Visits* (2013).

These make clear the expectation that the aims of the 2014 National Curriculum will underpin maths in schools.

*The responsibility of mathematics education is to enable all pupils to develop conceptual understanding of the mathematics they learn, its structures and relationships, and fluent recall of mathematical knowledge and skills to equip them to solve familiar problems as well as tackling creatively the more complex and unfamiliar ones that lie ahead.*

(Ofsted 2012)

Concerns about maths as it is currently observed being taught in primary classrooms, expressed by Ofsted in these reports and at the Ofsted Better Maths conferences (2013), include:

- *Pupils are not made to think hard enough for themselves.*
- *Conceptual understanding and problem solving are underemphasised.*
- *Too often, teaching approaches focus on how, without understanding why, so that pupils have insecure foundations on which to build future learning.*
- *Many pupils spend too long working on straightforward questions, with*

problems located at the ends of exercises or set as extension tasks, so
that not all tackle them.

- *Wide in-school variation in teaching quality.*
- *Checking and probing understanding throughout the lesson and adapting teaching accordingly are not strong enough.*
- *Teachers are not clear enough about progression, so teaching is fragmented and does not link concepts.*
- *Too much teaching concentrates on the acquisition of disparate skills that enable pupils to pass tests, but do not equip them for the next stage of education, work and life.*

They describe highly effective practice, where *teachers get 'inside pupils' heads'. They find out how pupils think by observing pupils closely, listening carefully to what they say and asking probing questions to extend their understanding, then adapting teaching accordingly.*

(Ofsted 2013)

Cross-curricular links are also identified as part of outstanding provision, in relation to the quality of the curriculum in mathematics:

*Links with other subjects in the school are highly productive in strengthening pupils' learning in mathematics. Rigorous curriculum planning ensures that mathematics makes an outstanding contribution to pupils' spiritual, moral, social and cultural development.*

(Ofsted 2013)

## Lesson observations

At the Better Mathematics conferences (Ofsted 2013), the following were identified as important areas to focus on during lesson observations: progress (the overarching focus that the other areas contribute to), monitoring to enhance progress, conceptual understanding, problem solving, misconceptions and accurate language and symbols. Subject leaders could use this list when observing lessons and focus on both the quality of the teacher input and the impact on pupils in each area.

## Work scrutiny

The focus from Ofsted, in relation to work scrutiny, again places importance on problem solving, conceptual understanding and assessment for learning.

*To check and improve:*
- *teaching approaches, including development of conceptual understanding*
- *depth and breadth of work set and tackled*
- *levels of challenge*
- *problem solving*
- *pupils' understanding and misconceptions*
- *assessment and its impact on understanding.*

*To look back over time and across year groups at:*
- *progression through concepts for pupils of different abilities*
- *how well pupils have overcome any earlier misconceptions*
- *balance and depth of coverage of the scheme of work, including using and applying mathematics.*

(Ofsted 2013)

# Managing the move towards the new National Curriculum: A checklist for mathematics subject leaders

## First steps

- Become familiar with the mathematics National Curriculum and the changes outlined above.
- Focus on the aims of the mathematics National Curriculum and ensure all teachers and teaching assistants understand them. Explore how these aims are currently reflected in the principles underpinning mathematics teaching in your school. Articulate the values, aims and principles you are starting from in a statement created with all staff.
- Ensure that all teachers understand that the curriculum is statutory only at the key-stage level and recognise the implications of this, including the need to look beyond a single year-group and the opportunity for shaping the curriculum.

## Following on

Consider: *What does the mathematics curriculum look like in our school?*

- Audit maths across the school and identify key areas for development linked to the new curriculum. Plan CPD for the whole staff which will have the greatest impact on pupils.
- Review your calculation policy and ensure that it reflects the principles underpinning mathematics in your school and the expectations of both the aims and the content of the curriculum. This will provide an opportunity to start shaping the curriculum and agreeing progression in a key area. Ensure that the policy includes key images to support understanding, expectations around language and decision making at all stages.
- Explore how you currently plan a route through the curriculum and how this will need to change, enabling clear connections to be made between different Domains, learning to be built on and expectations to be met. Lead staff in shaping the curriculum in line with agreed principles and the design of the whole curriculum.
- Examine the planning of teaching sequences; look for clear success criteria which are underpinned by the aims, and the identification of context, images, language and symbols that will be connected through the sequence.
- Audit maths resources and ensure that images are available to support understanding of concepts and explanation of thinking at all ages. In particular, focus on key images to support number and calculation. Look at how resources are used and accessed by the pupils as well as the adults.
- Investigate how talk is developed in maths classrooms.
- Look at how cross-curricular links are made and opportunities for maths across the curriculum are utilised.

## Monitoring the implementation of the new National Curriculum

- Talk with groups of pupils from across the school on a termly basis, concentrating on areas which have been the focus for development. Use this as an opportunity to probe conceptual understanding, assess talk and provide an opportunity for pupils to demonstrate their fluency, reasoning and problem-solving abilities.
- Observe teaching, again linked to areas which have been the focus for development.
- Review planning and pupils' books, focusing on one completed sequence of learning. Use a sample of pupils' work, including all books where they have used their mathematics and the Ofsted guidance on work scrutiny (see above).

## Evaluation

These key questions can be used to evaluate mathematics overall or a specific area of development, such as calculation:

- Are the aims of the curriculum evident as a key component of mathematics in the school?
- Is conceptual understanding being developed at all stages? Can pupils talk about and explain their mathematical thinking and understanding?
- Are pupils meeting age-related expectations as set out in the National Curriculum?
- Are there any gaps or underachieving groups?
- Are pupils making at least expected progress? Are enough making better than expected progress?
- Is the quality of mathematics teaching at least good or better?
- What further support and development is required?

# National Curriculum: Key Stages 1–2

## 1. Introduction

1.1 This document sets out the framework for the National Curriculum at Key Stages 1 and 2, and includes:

- contextual information about both the overall school curriculum and the statutory National Curriculum, including the statutory basis of the latter
- aims for the statutory National Curriculum
- statements on inclusion, and on the development of pupils' competence in numeracy and mathematics, language and literacy across the school curriculum
- Programmes of Study for mathematics at Key Stages 1 and 2.

## 2. The school curriculum in England

2.1 Every state-funded school must offer a curriculum which is balanced and broadly based[1] and which:

- promotes the spiritual, moral, cultural, mental and physical development of pupils at the school and of society, and
- prepares pupils at the school for the opportunities, responsibilities and experiences of later life.

2.2 The school curriculum comprises all learning and other experiences that each school plans for its pupils. The National Curriculum forms one part of the school curriculum.

2.3 All state schools are also required to make provision for a daily act of collective worship and must teach religious education to pupils at every key stage and sex and relationship education to pupils in secondary education.

2.4 Maintained schools in England are legally required to follow the statutory National Curriculum which sets out in Programmes of Study, on the basis of key stages, subject content for those subjects that should be taught to all pupils. All schools must publish their school curriculum by subject and academic year online[2].

2.5 All schools should make provision for personal, social, health and economic education (PSHE), drawing on good practice. Schools are also free to include other subjects or topics of their choice in planning and designing their own programme of education.

---

[1] See Section 78 of the 2002 Education Act: http://www.legislation.gov.uk/ukpga/2002/32/section/78 which applies to all maintained schools. Academies are also required to offer a broad and balanced curriculum in accordance with Section 1 of the 2010 Academies Act; http://www.legislation.gov.uk/ukpga/2010/32/section/1.

[2] From September 2012, all schools are required to publish information in relation to each academic year, relating to the content of the school's curriculum for each subject and details about how additional information relating to the curriculum may be obtained: http://www.legislation.gov.uk/uksi/2012/1124/made.

# 3. The National Curriculum in England

## Aims

3.1 The National Curriculum provides pupils with an introduction to the essential knowledge that they need to be educated citizens. It introduces pupils to the best that has been thought and said, and helps engender an appreciation of human creativity and achievement.

3.2 The National Curriculum is just one element in the education of every child. There is time and space in the school day and in each week, term and year to range beyond the National Curriculum specifications. The National Curriculum provides an outline of core knowledge around which teachers can develop exciting and stimulating lessons to promote the development of pupils' knowledge, understanding and skills as part of the wider school curriculum.

## Structure

3.3 Pupils of compulsory school age in community and foundation schools, including community special schools and foundation special schools, and in voluntary aided and voluntary controlled schools, must follow the National Curriculum. It is organised on the basis of four key stages[3] and twelve subjects, classified in legal terms as 'core' and 'other foundation' subjects.

3.4 The Secretary of State for Education is required to publish Programmes of Study for each National Curriculum subject, setting out the 'matters, skills and processes' to be taught at each key stage. Schools are free to choose how they organise their school day, as long as the content of National Curriculum Programmes of Study is taught to all pupils.

---

[3] The Key Stage 2 Programmes of Study for English, mathematics and science are presented in this document as 'lower' (Years 3 and 4) and 'upper' (Years 5 and 6). This distinction is made as guidance for teachers and is not reflected in legislation. The legal requirement is to cover the content of the Programmes of Study for Years 3 to 6 by the end of Key Stage 2.

3.5 The proposed structure of the new National Curriculum, in terms of which subjects are compulsory at each key stage, is set out in the table below:

*Figure 1 – Structure of the National Curriculum*

|  | Key Stage 1 | Key Stage 2 | Key Stage 3 | Key Stage 4 |
|---|---|---|---|---|
| **Age** | 5–7 | 7–11 | 11–14 | 14–16 |
| **Year groups** | 1–2 | 3–6 | 7–9 | 10–11 |
| **Core subjects** |  |  |  |  |
| English | ✓ | ✓ | ✓ | ✓ |
| Mathematics | ✓ | ✓ | ✓ | ✓ |
| Science | ✓ | ✓ | ✓ | ✓ |
| **Foundation subjects** |  |  |  |  |
| Art and design | ✓ | ✓ | ✓ |  |
| Citizenship |  |  | ✓ | ✓ |
| Computing | ✓ | ✓ | ✓ | ✓ |
| Design and technology | ✓ | ✓ | ✓ |  |
| Languages[4] |  | ✓ | ✓ |  |
| Geography | ✓ | ✓ | ✓ |  |
| History | ✓ | ✓ | ✓ |  |
| Music | ✓ | ✓ | ✓ |  |
| Physical education | ✓ | ✓ | ✓ | ✓ |

3.6 All schools are also required to teach religious education at all key stages.

Secondary schools must provide sex and relationship education.

*Figure 2 – Statutory teaching of religious education and sex and relationship education*

|  | Key Stage 1 | Key Stage 2 | Key Stage 3 | Key Stage 4 |
|---|---|---|---|---|
| **Age** |  | 7–11 | 11–14 | 14–16 |
| **Year groups** | 1–2 | 3–6 | 7–9 | 10–11 |
| Religious education | ✓ | ✓ | ✓ | ✓ |
| Sex and relationship education |  |  | ✓ | ✓ |

---

[4] At Key Stage 2 the subject title is 'foreign language'; at key stage 3 it is 'modern foreign language'.

# 4. Inclusion

## Setting suitable challenges

4.1 Teachers should set high expectations for every pupil. They should plan stretching work for pupils whose attainment is significantly above the expected standard. They have an even greater obligation to plan lessons for pupils who have low levels of prior attainment or come from disadvantaged backgrounds. Teachers should use appropriate assessment to set targets which are deliberately ambitious.

## Responding to pupils' needs and overcoming potential barriers for individuals and groups of pupils

4.2 Teachers should take account of their duties under equal opportunities legislation that covers race, disability, sex, religion or belief, sexual orientation, pregnancy and maternity, and gender assessment.

4.3 A wide range of pupils have special educational needs, many of whom also have disabilities. Lessons should be planned to ensure that there are no barriers to every child achieving. In many cases, such planning will mean that these pupils will be able to study the full National Curriculum. The SEN Code of Practice will include advice on approaches to identification of need which can support this. A minority of pupils will need access to specialist equipment and different approaches. The SEN Code of Practice will outline what needs to be done for them.

4.4 With the right teaching that recognises their individual needs, many disabled pupils have little need for additional resources beyond the aids which they use as part of their daily life. Teachers must plan lessons so that these pupils can study every National Curriculum subject. Potential areas of difficulty should be identified and addressed at the outset of work.

4.5 Teachers must also take account of the needs of pupils whose first language is not English. Monitoring of progress should take account of the child's age, length of time in this country, previous educational experience and ability in other languages.

4.6 The ability of pupils for whom English is an additional language to take part in the National Curriculum may be in advance of their communication skills in English. Teachers should plan teaching opportunities to help pupils develop their English and should aim to provide the support pupils need to take part in all subjects.

---

[5] Age is a protected characteristic under the Equality Act 2010 but it is not applicable to schools in relation to education or (as far as relating to those under the age of 18) the provision of services; it is a relevant protected characteristic in relation to the provision of services or employment (so when thinking about staff). Marriage and civil partnership are also a protected characteristic but only in relation to employment.

# 5. Numeracy and mathematics

5.1 Teachers should use every relevant subject to develop pupils' mathematical fluency. Confidence in numeracy and other mathematical skills is a precondition of success across the National Curriculum

5.2 Teachers should develop pupils' numeracy and mathematical reasoning in all subjects so that they understand and appreciate the importance of mathematics. Pupils should be taught to apply arithmetic fluently to problems, understand and use measures, make estimates and sense check their work. Pupils should apply their geometric and algebraic understanding, and relate their understanding of probability to the notions of risk and uncertainty. They should also understand the cycle of collecting, presenting and analysing data. They should be taught to apply their mathematics to both routine and non-routine problems, including breaking down more complex problems into a series of simpler steps.

# 6. Language and literacy

6.1 Teachers should develop pupils' spoken language, reading, writing and vocabulary as integral aspects of the teaching of every subject. English is both a subject in its own right and the medium for teaching; for pupils, understanding the language provides access to the whole curriculum. Fluency in the English language is an essential foundation for success in all subjects.

## Spoken language

6.2 Pupils should be taught to speak clearly and convey ideas confidently using Standard English. They should learn to justify ideas with reasons; ask questions to check understanding; develop vocabulary and build knowledge; negotiate; evaluate and build on the ideas of others; and select the appropriate register for effective communication. They should be taught to give well-structured descriptions and explanations and develop their understanding through speculating, hypothesising and exploring ideas. This will enable them to clarify their thinking as well as organise their ideas for writing.

## Reading and writing

6.3 Teachers should develop pupils' reading and writing in all subjects to support their acquisition of knowledge. Pupils should be taught to read fluently, understand extended prose (both fiction and non-fiction) and be encouraged to read for pleasure. Schools should do everything to promote wider reading. They should provide library facilities and set ambitious expectations for reading at home. Pupils should develop the stamina and skills to write at length, with accurate spelling and punctuation. They should be taught the correct use of grammar. They should build on what they have been taught to expand the range of their writing and the variety of the grammar they use. The writing they do should include narratives, explanations, descriptions, comparisons, summaries and evaluations: such writing supports them in rehearsing, understanding and consolidating what they have heard or read.

## Vocabulary development

6.4 Pupils' acquisition and command of vocabulary are key to their learning and progress across the whole curriculum. Teachers should therefore develop vocabulary actively, building systematically on pupils' current knowledge. They should increase pupils' store of words in general; simultaneously, they should also make links between known and new vocabulary and discuss the shades of meaning in similar words. In this way, pupils expand the vocabulary choices that are available to them when they write. In addition, it is vital for pupils' comprehension that they understand the meanings of words they meet in their reading across all subjects, and older pupils should be taught the meaning of instruction verbs that they may meet in examination questions. It is particularly important to induct pupils into the language which defines each subject in its own right, such as accurate mathematical and scientific language.

# 7. Programmes of Study and Attainment targets

7.1 The following pages set out the proposed statutory Programmes of Study for mathematics at Key Stages 1–2. Where content is shown in grey text, it is 'non-statutory'.

# Mathematics Programme of Study: Key Stages 1–2

## Purpose of study

Mathematics is a creative and highly interconnected discipline that has been developed over centuries, providing the solution to some of history's most intriguing problems. It is essential to everyday life, critical to science, technology and engineering, and necessary for financial literacy and most forms of employment. A high-quality mathematics education therefore provides a foundation for understanding the world, the ability to reason mathematically, an appreciation of the beauty and power of mathematics, and a sense of enjoyment and curiosity about the subject.

## Aims

The National Curriculum for mathematics aims to ensure that all pupils:

- become **fluent** in the fundamentals of mathematics, including through varied and frequent practice with increasingly complex problems over time, so that pupils develop conceptual understanding and the ability to recall and apply knowledge rapidly and accurately

- **reason mathematically** by following a line of enquiry, conjecturing relationships and generalisations, and developing an argument, justification or proof using mathematical language

- can **solve problems** by applying their mathematics to a variety of routine and non-routine problems with increasing sophistication, including breaking down problems into a series of simpler steps and persevering in seeking solutions.

Mathematics is an interconnected subject in which pupils need to be able to move fluently between representations of mathematical ideas. The Programmes of Study are, by necessity, organised into apparently distinct Domains, but pupils should make rich connections across mathematical ideas to develop fluency, mathematical reasoning and competence in solving increasingly sophisticated problems. They should also apply their mathematical knowledge to science and other subjects.

The expectation is that the majority of pupils will move through the Programmes of Study at broadly the same pace. However, decisions about when to progress should always be based on the security of pupils' understanding and their readiness to progress to the next stage. Pupils who grasp concepts rapidly should be challenged through being offered rich and sophisticated problems before any acceleration through new content. Those who are not sufficiently fluent with earlier material should consolidate their understanding, including through additional practice, before moving on.

## Information and communication technology (ICT)

Calculators should not be used as a substitute for good written and mental arithmetic. They should therefore only be introduced near the end of Key Stage 2 to support pupils' conceptual understanding and exploration of more complex number problems, if written and mental arithmetic are secure. In both primary and secondary schools, teachers should use their judgement about when ICT tools should be used.

## Spoken language

The National Curriculum for mathematics reflects the importance of spoken language in pupils' development across the whole curriculum – cognitively, socially and linguistically. The quality and variety of language that pupils hear and speak are key factors in developing their mathematical vocabulary and presenting a mathematical justification, argument or proof. They must be assisted in making their thinking clear to themselves as well as others, and teachers should ensure that pupils build secure foundations by using discussion to probe and remedy their misconceptions.

## School curriculum

The Programmes of Study for mathematics are set out year-by-year for Key Stages 1 and 2. Schools are, however, only required to teach the relevant Programme of Study by the end of the key stage. Within each key stage, schools therefore have the flexibility to introduce content earlier or later than set out in the Programme of Study. In addition, schools can introduce key stage content during an earlier key stage, if appropriate. All schools are also required to set out their school curriculum for mathematics on a year-by-year basis and make this information available online.

## Attainment targets

By the end of each key stage, pupils are expected to know, apply and understand the matters, skills and processes specified in the relevant Programme of Study.

**Schools are not required by law to teach the example content in grey tint or the content indicated as being non-statutory.**

## Key Stage 1 – Years 1 and 2

The principal focus of mathematics teaching in Key Stage 1 is to ensure that pupils develop confidence and mental fluency with whole numbers, counting and place value. This should involve working with numerals, words and the four operations, including with practical resources (for example, concrete objects and measuring tools).

At this stage, pupils should develop their ability to recognise, describe, draw, compare and sort different shapes and use the related vocabulary. Teaching should also involve using a range of measures to describe and compare different quantities such as length, mass, capacity/volume, time and money.

By the end of Year 2, pupils should know the number bonds to 20 and be precise in using and understanding place value. An emphasis on practice at this early stage will aid fluency.

Pupils should read and spell mathematical vocabulary, at a level consistent with their increasing word reading and spelling knowledge at Key Stage 1.

# Year 1

| Year 1 Programme of Study (statutory requirements) | Notes and guidance (non-statutory) |
|---|---|
| **NUMBER**<br><br>**Number and place value**<br><br>Pupils should be taught to:<br><br>• count to and across 100, forwards and backwards, beginning with 0 or 1, or from any given number<br><br>• count, read and write numbers to 100 in numerals; count in multiples of twos, fives and tens<br><br>• given a number, identify one more and one less<br><br>• identify and represent numbers using objects and pictorial representations including the number line, and use the language of: equal to, more than, less than (fewer), most, least<br><br>• read and write numbers from 1 to 20 in numerals and words. | **NUMBER**<br><br>**Number and place value**<br><br>Pupils practise counting (1, 2, 3), ordering (eg first, second, third), or to indicate a quantity (eg 3 apples, 2 centimetres), including solving simple concrete problems, until they are fluent.<br><br>Pupils begin to recognise place value in numbers beyond 20 by reading, writing, counting and comparing numbers up to 100, supported by objects and pictorial representations.<br><br>They practise counting as reciting numbers and counting as enumerating objects, and counting in twos, fives and tens from different multiples to develop their recognition of patterns in the number system (eg odd and even numbers), including varied and frequent practice through increasingly complex questions.<br><br>They recognise and create repeating patterns with objects and with shapes. |
| **Number: Addition and subtraction**<br><br>Pupils should be taught to:<br><br>• read, write and interpret mathematical statements involving addition (+), subtraction (−) and equals (=) signs<br><br>• represent and use number bonds and related subtraction facts within 20<br><br>• add and subtract one-digit and two-digit numbers to 20, including zero<br><br>• solve one-step problems that involve addition and subtraction, using concrete objects and pictorial representations, and missing number problems such as 7 = □ − 9. | **Addition and subtraction**<br><br>Pupils memorise and reason with number bonds to 10 and 20 in several forms (eg 9 + 7 = 16; 16 − 7 = 9; 7 = 16 − 9). They should realise the effect of adding or subtracting zero. This establishes addition and subtraction as related operations.<br><br>Pupils combine and increase numbers, counting forwards and backwards.<br><br>They discuss and solve problems in familiar practical contexts, including using quantities. Problems should include the terms: put together, add, altogether, total, take away, distance between, difference between, more than and less than, so that pupils develop the concept of addition and subtraction and are enabled to use these operations flexibly. |

| Year 1 Programme of Study (statutory requirements) | Notes and guidance (non-statutory) |
|---|---|
| **Number: Multiplication and division**<br><br>Pupils should be taught to:<br><br>• solve one-step problems involving multiplication and division, by calculating the answer using concrete objects, pictorial representations and arrays with the support of the teacher. | **Multiplication and division**<br><br>Through grouping and sharing small quantities, pupils begin to understand: multiplication and division; doubling numbers and quantities; and finding simple fractions of objects, numbers and quantities.<br><br>They make connections between arrays, number patterns, and counting in twos, fives and tens. |
| **Number: Fractions**<br><br>Pupils should be taught to:<br><br>• recognise, find and name a half as one of two equal parts of an object, shape or quantity<br><br>• recognise, find and name a quarter as one of four equal parts of an object, shape or quantity. | **Fractions**<br><br>Pupils are taught half and quarter as 'fractions of' discrete and continuous quantities by solving problems using shapes, objects and quantities. For example, they could recognise and find half a length, quantity, set of objects or shape. Pupils connect halves and quarters to the equal sharing and grouping of sets of objects and to measures, as well as recognising and combining halves and quarters as parts of a whole. |
| **MEASUREMENT**<br><br>Pupils should be taught to:<br><br>• compare, describe and solve practical problems for:<br><br>  • lengths and heights (for example, long/short, longer/shorter, tall/short, double/half)<br><br>  • mass or weight (for example, heavy/light, heavier than, lighter than)<br><br>  • capacity and volume (for example, full/empty, more than, less than, half, half full, quarter)<br><br>  • time (for example, quicker, slower, earlier, later)<br><br>• measure and begin to record the following:<br><br>  • lengths and heights<br><br>  • mass/weight<br><br>  • capacity and volume<br><br>  • time (hours, minutes, seconds)<br><br>• recognise and know the value of different denominations of coins and notes | **MEASUREMENT**<br><br>The pairs of terms: mass and weight, volume and capacity, are used interchangeably at this stage.<br><br>Pupils move from using and comparing different types of quantities and measures using non-standard units, including discrete (eg counting) and continuous (eg liquid) measurement, to using manageable common standard units.<br><br>In order to become familiar with standard measures, pupils begin to use measuring tools such as a ruler, weighing scales and containers.<br><br>Pupils use the language of time, including telling the time throughout the day, first using o'clock and then half past. |

| Year 1 Programme of Study (statutory requirements) | Notes and guidance (non-statutory) |
|---|---|
| • sequence events in chronological order using language (for example, before and after, next, first, today, yesterday, tomorrow, morning, afternoon and evening) | |
| • recognise and use language relating to dates, including days of the week, weeks, months and years | |
| • tell the time to the hour and half past the hour and draw the hands on a clock face to show these times. | |
| **GEOMETRY** **Properties of shapes** Pupils should be taught to: | **GEOMETRY** **Properties of shapes** Pupils handle common 2D and 3D shapes, naming these and related everyday objects fluently. They recognise these shapes in different orientations and sizes, and know that rectangles, triangles, cuboids and pyramids are not always similar to each other. |
| • recognise and name common 2D and 3D shapes, including: | |
|   • 2D shapes (for example, rectangles (including squares), circles and triangles) | |
|   • 3D shapes (for example, cuboids (including cubes), pyramids and spheres). | |
| **Geometry: Position and direction** Pupils should be taught to: | **Position and direction** Pupils use the language of position, direction and motion, including: left and right, top, middle and bottom, on top of, in front of, above, between, around, near, close and far, up and down, forwards and backwards, inside and outside. |
| • describe position, directions and movements, including whole, half, quarter and three-quarter turns. | Pupils make whole, half, quarter and three-quarter turns in both directions and connect turning clockwise with movement on a clock face. |

# Year 2

| Year 2 Programme of Study (statutory requirements) | Notes and guidance (non-statutory) |
|---|---|
| **NUMBER**<br>**Number and place value**<br>Pupils should be taught to:<br><br>• count in steps of 2, 3 and 5 from 0, and in tens from any number, forward or backward<br>• recognise the place value of each digit in a two-digit number (tens, ones)<br>• identify, represent and estimate numbers using different representations, including the number line<br>• compare and order numbers from 0 up to 100; use <, > and = signs<br>• read and write numbers to at least 100 in numerals and in words<br>• use place value and number facts to solve problems. | **NUMBER**<br>**Number and place value**<br>Using materials and a range of representations, pupils practise counting, reading, writing and comparing numbers to at least 100 and solving a variety of related problems to develop fluency. They count in multiples of three to support their later understanding of a third.<br><br>As they become more confident with numbers up to 100, pupils are introduced to larger numbers to develop further their recognition of patterns within the number system and represent them in different ways, including spatial representations.<br><br>Pupils should partition numbers in different ways (for example, 23 = 20 + 3 and 23 = 10 + 13) to support subtraction. They become fluent and apply their knowledge of numbers to reason with, discuss and solve problems that emphasise the value of each digit in two-digit numbers. They begin to understand zero as a placeholder. |
| **Number: Addition and subtraction**<br>Pupils should be taught to:<br><br>• solve problems with addition and subtraction:<br>  • using concrete objects and pictorial representations, including those involving numbers, quantities and measures<br>  • applying their increasing knowledge of mental and written methods<br>• recall and use addition and subtraction facts to 20 fluently, and derive and use related facts up to 100<br>• add and subtract numbers using concrete objects, pictorial representations, and mentally, including:<br>  • a two-digit number and ones<br>  • a two-digit number and tens<br>  • two two-digit numbers<br>  • adding three one-digit numbers | **Addition and subtraction**<br>Pupils extend their understanding of the language of addition and subtraction to include sum and difference.<br><br>Pupils practise addition and subtraction to 20 to become increasingly fluent in deriving facts, such as using $3 + 7 = 10$, $10 − 7 = 3$ and $7 = 10 − 3$ to calculate $30 + 70 = 100$, $100 − 70 = 30$ and $70 = 100 − 30$. They check their calculations, including by adding to check subtraction and adding numbers in a different order to check addition (for example, $5 + 2 + 1 = 1 + 5 + 2 = 1 + 2 + 5$). This establishes commutativity and associativity of addition.<br><br>Recording addition and subtraction in columns supports place value and prepares for formal written methods with larger numbers. |

| Year 2 Programme of Study (statutory requirements) | Notes and guidance (non-statutory) |
|---|---|
| • show that addition of two numbers can be done in any order (commutative) and subtraction of one number from another cannot<br>• recognise and use the inverse relationship between addition and subtraction and use this to check calculations and solve missing number problems.<br><br>**Number: Multiplication and division**<br>Pupils should be taught to:<br>• recall and use multiplication and division facts for the 2, 5 and 10 multiplication tables, including recognising odd and even numbers<br>• calculate mathematical statements for multiplication and division within the multiplication tables and write them using the multiplication (×), division (÷) and equals (=) signs<br>• show that multiplication of two numbers can be done in any order (commutative) and division of one number by another cannot<br>• solve problems involving multiplication and division, using materials, arrays, repeated addition, mental methods, and multiplication and division facts, including problems in contexts.<br><br>**Number: Fractions**<br>Pupils should be taught to:<br>• recognise, find, name and write fractions $\frac{1}{3}$, $\frac{1}{4}$, $\frac{2}{4}$ and $\frac{3}{4}$ of a length, shape, set of objects or quantity<br>• write simple fractions eg $\frac{1}{2}$ of 6 = 3 and recognise the equivalence of $\frac{2}{4}$ and $\frac{1}{2}$. | **Multiplication and division**<br>Pupils use a variety of language to describe multiplication and division.<br><br>Pupils are introduced to the multiplication tables. They practise to become fluent in the 2, 5 and 10 multiplication tables and connect them to each other. They connect the 10 multiplication table to place value, and the 5 multiplication table to the divisions on the clock face. They begin to use other multiplication tables and recall multiplication facts, including using related division facts to perform written and mental calculations.<br><br>Pupils work with a range of materials and contexts in which multiplication and division relate to grouping and sharing discrete and continuous quantities, to arrays and to repeated addition. They begin to relate these to fractions and measures (for example, $40 \div 2 = 20$, 20 is a half of 40). They use commutativity and inverse relations to develop multiplicative reasoning (for example, $4 \times 5 = 20$ and $20 \div 5 = 4$).<br><br>**Fractions**<br>Pupils use fractions as 'fractions of' discrete and continuous quantities by solving problems using shapes, objects and quantities. They connect unit fractions to equal sharing and grouping, to numbers when they can be calculated, and to measures, finding fractions of lengths, quantity, a set of objects or shapes. They meet $\frac{3}{4}$ as the first example of a non-unit fraction.<br><br>Pupils should count in fractions up to 10, starting from any number and using the $\frac{1}{2}$ and $\frac{2}{4}$ equivalence on the number line (for example, $1\frac{1}{4}$, $1\frac{2}{4}$ (or $1\frac{1}{2}$), $1\frac{3}{4}$, 2). This reinforces the concept of fractions as numbers and that they can add up to more than one. |

| Year 2 Programme of Study (statutory requirements) | Notes and guidance (non-statutory) |
|---|---|
| **MEASUREMENT** | **MEASUREMENT** |
| Pupils should be taught to: | Pupils use standard units of measurement with increasing accuracy, using their knowledge of the number system. They use the appropriate language and record using standard abbreviations. |
| • choose and use appropriate standard units to estimate and measure length/height in any direction (m/cm); mass (kg/g); temperature (°C); capacity (litres/ml) to the nearest appropriate unit, using rulers, scales, thermometers and measuring vessels | Comparing measures includes simple multiples such as 'half as high'; 'twice as wide'. |
| • compare and order lengths, mass, volume/capacity and record the results using >, < and = | They become fluent in telling the time on analogue clocks and recording it. |
| • recognise and use symbols for pounds (£) and pence (p); combine amounts to make a particular value | Pupils become fluent in counting and recognising coins. They read and say amounts of money confidently and use the symbols £ and p accurately, recording pounds and pence separately. |
| • find different combinations of coins that equal the same amounts of money | |
| • solve simple problems in a practical context involving addition and subtraction of money of the same unit, including giving change | |
| • compare and sequence intervals of time | |
| • tell and write the time to five minutes, including quarter past/to the hour and draw the hands on a clock face to show these times | |
| • know the number of minutes in an hour and the number of hours in a day. | |
| **GEOMETRY** | **GEOMETRY** |
| **Properties of shapes** | **Properties of shapes** |
| Pupils should be taught to: | Pupils handle and name a wider variety of common 2D and 3D shapes including: quadrilaterals and polygons, and cuboids, prisms and cones, and identify the properties of each shape (eg number of sides, number of faces). Pupils identify, compare and sort shapes on the basis of their properties and use vocabulary precisely, such as sides, edges, vertices and faces. |
| • identify and describe the properties of 2D shapes, including the number of sides and line symmetry in a vertical line | Pupils read and write names for shapes that are appropriate for their word reading and spelling. |
| • identify and describe the properties of 3D shapes, including the number of edges, vertices and faces | Pupils draw lines and shapes using a straight edge. |
| • identify 2D shapes on the surface of 3D shapes, (for example a circle on a cylinder and a triangle on a pyramid) | |
| • compare and sort common 2D and 3D shapes and everyday objects. | |

## Year 2 Programme of Study (statutory requirements)

### Geometry: Position and direction

Pupils should be taught to:

- order and arrange combinations of mathematical objects in patterns and sequences

- use mathematical vocabulary to describe position, direction and movement, including movement in a straight line and distinguishing between rotation as a turn and in terms of right angles for quarter, half and three-quarter turns (clockwise and anti-clockwise).

### STATISTICS

Pupils should be taught to:

- interpret and construct simple pictograms, tally charts, block diagrams and simple tables

- ask and answer simple questions by counting the number of objects in each category and sorting the categories by quantity

- ask and answer questions about totalling and comparing categorical data.

## Notes and guidance (non-statutory)

### Position and direction

Pupils should work with patterns of shapes, including those in different orientations.

Pupils use the concept and language of angles to describe 'turn' by applying rotations, including in practical contexts (for example, pupils themselves moving in turns, giving instructions to other pupils to do so, and programming robots using instructions given in right angles).

### STATISTICS

Pupils record, interpret, collate, organise and compare information (for example, using many-to-one correspondence with simple ratios 2, 5, 10).

# Lower Key Stage 2 – Years 3 and 4

The principal focus of mathematics teaching in lower Key Stage 2 is to ensure that pupils become increasingly fluent with whole numbers and the four operations, including number facts and the concept of place value. This should ensure that pupils develop efficient written and mental methods and perform calculations accurately with increasingly large whole numbers.

At this stage, pupils should develop their ability to solve a range of problems, including with simple fractions and decimal place value. Teaching should also ensure that pupils draw with increasing accuracy and develop mathematical reasoning so they can analyse shapes and their properties, and confidently describe the relationships between them. It should ensure that they can use measuring instruments with accuracy and make connections between measure and number.

By the end of Year 4, pupils should have memorised their multiplication tables up to and including the 12 multiplication table and show precision and fluency in their work.

Pupils should read and spell mathematical vocabulary correctly and confidently, using their growing word reading knowledge and their knowledge of spelling.

# Year 3

| Year 3 Programme of Study (statutory requirements) | Notes and guidance (non-statutory) |
|---|---|
| **NUMBER** | **NUMBER** |
| **Number and place value** | **Number and place value** |
| Pupils should be taught to: | Pupils now use multiples of 2, 3, 4, 5, 8, 10, 50 and 100. |
| • count from 0 in multiples of 4, 8, 50 and 100; find 10 or 100 more or less than a given number | They use larger numbers to at least 1000, applying partitioning related to place value using varied and increasingly complex problems, building on work in Year 2 (for example, 146 = 100 + 40 and 6, 146 = 130 + 16). |
| • recognise the place value of each digit in a three-digit number (hundreds, tens, ones) | Using a variety of representations, including those related to measure, pupils continue to count in ones, tens and hundreds, so that they become fluent in the order and place value of numbers to 1000. |
| • compare and order numbers up to 1000 | |
| • identify, represent and estimate numbers using different representations | |
| • read and write numbers up to 1000 in numerals and in words | |
| • solve number problems and practical problems involving these ideas. | |
| **Number: Addition and subtraction** | **Addition and subtraction** |
| Pupils should be taught to: | Pupils practise solving varied addition and subtraction questions. For mental calculations with two-digit numbers, the answers could exceed 100. |
| • add and subtract numbers mentally, including: | Pupils use their understanding of place value and partitioning, and practise using columnar addition and subtraction with increasingly large numbers up to three digits to become fluent (see Mathematics Appendix 1). |
|   • a three-digit number and ones | |
|   • a three-digit number and tens | |
|   • a three-digit number and hundreds | |
| • add and subtract numbers with up to three digits, using formal written methods of columnar addition and subtraction | |
| • estimate the answer to a calculation and use inverse operations to check answers | |
| • solve problems, including missing number problems, using number facts, place value, and more complex addition and subtraction. | |

# Year 3 Programme of Study (statutory requirements)

## Number: Multiplication and division

Pupils should be taught to:

- recall and use multiplication and division facts for the 3, 4 and 8 multiplication tables

- write and calculate mathematical statements for multiplication and division using the multiplication tables that they know, including for two-digit numbers times one-digit numbers, using mental and progressing to formal written methods

- solve problems, including missing number problems, involving multiplication and division, including positive integer scaling problems and correspondence problems in which *n* objects are connected to *m* objects.

# Notes and guidance (non-statutory)

## Multiplication and division

Pupils continue to practise their mental recall of multiplication tables when they are calculating mathematical statements in order to improve fluency. Through doubling, they connect the 2, 4 and 8 multiplication tables.

Pupils develop efficient mental methods, for example, using commutativity and associativity (for example, $4 \times 12 \times 5 = 4 \times 5 \times 12 = 20 \times 12 = 240$) and multiplication and division facts (for example, using $3 \times 2 = 6$, $6 \div 3 = 2$ and $2 = 6 \div 3$) to derive related facts (for example, $30 \times 2 = 60$, $60 \div 3 = 20$ and $20 = 60 \div 3$).

Pupils develop reliable written methods for multiplication and division, starting with calculations of two-digit numbers by one-digit numbers and progressing to the formal written methods of short multiplication and division.

Pupils solve simple problems in contexts, deciding which of the four operations to use and why. These include measuring and scaling contexts, (for example, four times as high, eight times as long etc.) and correspondence problems in which *m* objects are connected to *n* objects (for example, 3 hats and 4 coats, how many different outfits?; 12 sweets shared equally between 4 children; 4 cakes shared equally between 8 children).

## Year 3 Programme of Study (statutory requirements)

### Number: Fractions

Pupils should be taught to:

- count up and down in tenths; recognise that tenths arise from dividing an object into 10 equal parts and in dividing one-digit numbers or quantities by 10
- recognise, find and write fractions of a discrete set of objects: unit fractions and non-unit fractions with small denominators
- recognise and use fractions as numbers: unit fractions and non-unit fractions with small denominators
- recognise and show, using diagrams, equivalent fractions with small denominators
- add and subtract fractions with the same denominator within one whole (for example, $5/7 + 1/7 = 6/7$)
- compare and order unit fractions, and fractions with the same denominators
- solve problems that involve all of the above.

### MEASUREMENT

Pupils should be taught to:

- measure, compare, add and subtract: lengths (m/cm/mm); mass (kg/g); volume/capacity (l/ml)
- measure the perimeter of simple 2D shapes
- add and subtract amounts of money to give change, using both £ and p in practical contexts
- tell and write the time from an analogue clock, including using Roman numerals from I to XII, and 12-hour and 24-hour clocks
- estimate and read time with increasing accuracy to the nearest minute; record and compare time in terms of seconds, minutes, and hours; use vocabulary such as o'clock, a.m./p.m., morning, afternoon, noon and midnight
- know the number of seconds in a minute and the number of days in each month, year and leap year
- compare durations of events, (for example to calculate the time taken by particular events or tasks).

## Notes and guidance (non-statutory)

### Fractions

Pupils connect tenths to place value, decimal measures and to division by 10.

They begin to understand unit and non-unit fractions as numbers on the number line, and deduce relations between them, such as size and equivalence. They should go beyond the [0, 1] interval, including relating this to measure.

Pupils understand the relation between unit fractions as operators (fractions of), and division by integers.

They continue to recognise fractions in the context of parts of a whole, numbers, measurements, a shape, and unit fractions as a division of a quantity.

Pupils practise adding and subtracting fractions with the same denominator through a variety of increasingly complex problems to improve fluency.

### MEASUREMENT

Pupils continue to measure using the appropriate tools and units, progressing to using a wider range of measures, including comparing and using mixed units (for example, 1kg and 200g) and simple equivalents of mixed units (for example, 5m = 500cm).

The comparison of measures includes simple scaling by integers (for example, a given quantity or measure is twice as long or five times as high) and this connects to multiplication.

Pupils continue to become fluent in recognising the value of coins, by adding and subtracting amounts, including mixed units, and giving change using manageable amounts. They record £ and p separately. The decimal recording of money is introduced formally in Year 4.

Pupils use both analogue and digital 12-hour clocks and record their times. In this way they become fluent in and prepared for using digital 24-hour clocks in Year 4.

| Year 3 Programme of Study (statutory requirements) | Notes and guidance (non-statutory) |
|---|---|
| **GEOMETRY**<br><br>**Properties of shapes**<br><br>Pupils should be taught to:<br><br>• draw 2D shapes and make 3D shapes using modelling materials; recognise 3D shapes in different orientations and describe them<br><br>• recognise angles as a property of shape or a description of a turn<br><br>• identify right angles, recognise that two right angles make a half-turn, three make three quarters of a turn and four a complete turn; identify whether angles are greater than or less than a right angle<br><br>• identify horizontal and vertical lines and pairs of perpendicular and parallel lines. | **GEOMETRY**<br><br>**Properties of shapes**<br><br>Pupils' knowledge of the properties of shapes is extended at this stage to symmetrical and non-symmetrical polygons and polyhedra. Pupils extend their use of the properties of shapes. They should be able to describe the properties of 2D and 3D shapes using accurate language, including lengths of lines and acute and obtuse for angles greater or lesser than a right angle.<br><br>Pupils connect decimals and rounding to drawing and measuring straight lines in centimetres, in a variety of contexts. |
| **STATISTICS**<br><br>Pupils should be taught to:<br><br>• interpret and present data using bar charts, pictograms and tables<br><br>• solve one-step and two-step questions (for example, 'How many more?' and 'How many fewer?') using information presented in scaled bar charts and pictograms and tables. | **STATISTICS**<br><br>Pupils understand and use simple scales (for example, 2, 5, 10 units per cm) in pictograms and bar charts with increasing accuracy.<br><br>They continue to interpret data presented in many contexts. |

**■SCHOLASTIC**

# Year 4

| Year 4 Programme of Study (statutory requirements) | Notes and guidance (non-statutory) |
|---|---|
| **NUMBER**<br><br>**Number and place value**<br><br>Pupils should be taught to:<br><br>• count in multiples of 6, 7, 9, 25 and 1000<br><br>• find 1000 more or less than a given number<br><br>• count backwards through zero to include negative numbers<br><br>• recognise the place value of each digit in a four-digit number (thousands, hundreds, tens and ones)<br><br>• order and compare numbers beyond 1000<br><br>• identify, represent and estimate numbers using different representations<br><br>• round any number to the nearest 10, 100 or 1000<br><br>• solve number and practical problems that involve all of the above and with increasingly large positive numbers<br><br>• read Roman numerals to 100 (I to C) and know that over time, the numeral system changed to include the concept of zero and place value. | **NUMBER**<br><br>**Number and place value**<br><br>Using a variety of representations, including measures, pupils become fluent in the order and place value of numbers beyond 1000, including counting in tens and hundreds, and maintaining fluency in other multiples through varied and frequent practice.<br><br>They begin to extend their knowledge of the number system to include the decimal numbers and fractions that they have met so far.<br><br>They connect estimation and rounding numbers to the use of measuring instruments.<br><br>Roman numerals should be put in their historical context so pupils understand that there have been different ways to write whole numbers and that the important concepts of zero and place value were introduced over a period of time. |
| **Number: Addition and subtraction**<br><br>Pupils should be taught to:<br><br>• add and subtract numbers with up to 4 digits using the formal written methods of columnar addition and subtraction where appropriate<br><br>• estimate and use inverse operations to check answers to a calculation<br><br>• solve addition and subtraction two-step problems in contexts, deciding which operations and methods to use and why. | **Addition and subtraction**<br><br>Pupils continue to practise both mental methods and columnar addition and subtraction with increasingly large numbers to aid fluency (see Mathematics Appendix 1). |

| Year 4 Programme of Study (statutory requirements) | Notes and guidance (non-statutory) |
|---|---|
| **Number: Multiplication and division**<br><br>Pupils should be taught to:<br><br>• recall multiplication and division facts for multiplication tables up to 12 × 12<br><br>• use place value, known and derived facts to multiply and divide mentally, including: multiplying by 0 and 1; dividing by 1; multiplying together three numbers<br><br>• recognise and use factor pairs and commutativity in mental calculations<br><br>• multiply two-digit and three-digit numbers by a one-digit number using formal written layout<br><br>• solve problems involving multiplying and adding, including using the distributive law to multiply two-digit numbers by one digit, integer scaling problems and harder correspondence problems such as *n* objects are connected to *m* objects. | **Multiplication and division**<br><br>Pupils continue to practise recalling and using multiplication tables and related division facts to aid fluency.<br><br>Pupils practise mental methods and extend this to three-digit numbers to derive facts (for example $600 ÷ 3 = 200$ can be derived from $2 × 3 = 6$).<br><br>Pupils practise to become fluent in the formal written method of short multiplication and short division with exact answers (see Mathematics Appendix 1).<br><br>Pupils write statements about the equality of expressions (for example, use the distributive law $39 × 7 = 30 × 7 + 9 × 7$ and associative law $(2 × 3) × 4 = 2 × (3 × 4)$). They combine their knowledge of number facts and rules of arithmetic to solve mental and written calculations for example, $2 × 6 × 5 = 10 × 6$.<br><br>Pupils solve two-step problems in contexts, choosing the appropriate operation, working with increasingly harder numbers. This should include correspondence questions such as the numbers of choices of a meal on a menu, or three cakes shared equally between 10 children. |

## Year 4 Programme of Study (statutory requirements)

### Number: Fractions (including decimals)

Pupils should be taught to:

- recognise and show, using diagrams, families of common equivalent fractions

- count up and down in hundredths; recognise that hundredths arise when dividing an object by one hundred and dividing tenths by ten

- solve problems involving increasingly harder fractions to calculate quantities, and fractions to divide quantities, including non-unit fractions where the answer is a whole number

- add and subtract fractions with the same denominator

- recognise and write decimal equivalents of any number of tenths or hundredths

- recognise and write decimal equivalents to $\frac{1}{4}$; $\frac{1}{2}$; $\frac{3}{4}$

- find the effect of dividing a one- or two-digit number by 10 and 100, identifying the value of the digits in the answer as ones, tenths and hundredths

- round decimals with one decimal place to the nearest whole number

- compare numbers with the same number of decimal places up to two decimal places

- solve simple measure and money problems involving fractions and decimals to two decimal places.

## Notes and guidance (non-statutory)

### Fractions (including decimals)

Pupils should connect hundredths to tenths and place value and decimal measure.

They extend the use of the number line to connect fractions, numbers and measures.

Pupils understand the relation between non-unit fractions and multiplication and division of quantities, with particular emphasis on tenths and hundredths.

Pupils make connections between fractions of a length, of a shape and as a representation of one whole or set of quantities. Pupils use factors and multiples to recognise equivalent fractions and simplify where appropriate (for example, $\frac{6}{9} = \frac{2}{3}$ or $\frac{1}{4} = \frac{2}{8}$).

Pupils continue to practise adding and subtracting fractions with the same denominator, to become fluent through a variety of increasingly complex problems beyond one whole.

Pupils are taught throughout that decimals and fractions are different ways of expressing numbers and proportions.

Pupils' understanding of the number system and decimal place value is extended at this stage to tenths and then hundredths. This includes relating the decimal notation to division of whole number by 10 and later 100.

They practise counting using simple fractions and decimal fractions, both forwards and backwards.

Pupils learn decimal notation and the language associated with it, including in the context of measurements. They make comparisons and order decimal amounts and quantities that are expressed to the same number of decimal places. They should be able to represent numbers with one or two decimal places in several ways, such as on number lines.

## Year 4 Programme of Study (statutory requirements)

### MEASUREMENT

Pupils should be taught to:

- Convert between different units of measure (for example, kilometre to metre; hour to minute)

- measure and calculate the perimeter of a rectilinear figure (including squares) in centimetres and metres

- find the area of rectilinear shapes by counting squares

- estimate, compare and calculate different measures, including money in pounds and pence

- read, write and convert time between analogue and digital 12- and 24-hour clocks

- solve problems involving converting from hours to minutes; minutes to seconds; years to months; weeks to days.

### GEOMETRY

### Properties of shapes

Pupils should be taught to:

- compare and classify geometric shapes, including quadrilaterals and triangles, based on their properties and sizes

- identify acute and obtuse angles and compare and order angles up to two right angles by size

- identify lines of symmetry in 2D shapes presented in different orientations

- complete a simple symmetric figure with respect to a specific line of symmetry.

## Notes and guidance (non-statutory)

### MEASUREMENT

Pupils build on their understanding of place value and decimal notation to record metric measures, including money.

They use multiplication to convert from larger to smaller units.

Perimeter can be expressed algebraically as $2(a + b)$ where $a$ and $b$ are the dimensions in the same unit.

They relate area to arrays and multiplication.

### GEOMETRY

### Properties of shapes

Pupils continue to classify shapes using geometrical properties, extending to classifying different triangles (for example, isosceles, equilateral, scalene) and quadrilaterals (for example, parallelogram, rhombus, trapezium).

Pupils compare and order angles in preparation for using a protractor and compare lengths and angles to decide if a polygon is regular or irregular.

Pupils draw symmetric patterns using a variety of media to become familiar with different orientations of lines of symmetry; and recognise line symmetry in a variety of diagrams, including where the line of symmetry does not dissect the original shape.

| Year 4 Programme of Study (statutory requirements) | Notes and guidance (non-statutory) |
|---|---|
| **Geometry: Position and direction** | **Position and direction** |
| Pupils should be taught to: | Pupils draw a pair of axes in one quadrant, with equal scales and integer labels. They read, write and use pairs of coordinates for example (2, 5) including using coordinate-plotting ICT tools. |
| • describe positions on a 2D grid as coordinates in the first quadrant | |
| • describe movements between positions as translations of a given unit to the left/right and up/down | |
| • plot specified points and draw sides to complete a given polygon. | |
| **STATISTICS** | **STATISTICS** |
| Pupils should be taught to: | Pupils understand and use a greater range of scales in their representations. |
| • interpret and present discrete and continuous data using appropriate graphical methods, including bar charts and time graphs | Pupils begin to relate the graphical representation of data to recording change over time. |
| • solve comparison, sum and difference problems using information presented in bar charts, pictograms, tables and other graphs. | |

# Upper Key Stage 2 – Years 5 and 6

The principal focus of mathematics teaching in upper Key Stage 2 is to ensure that pupils extend their understanding of the number system and place value to include larger integers. This should develop the connections that pupils make between multiplication and division with fractions, decimals, percentages and ratio.

At this stage, pupils should develop their ability to solve a wider range of problems, including increasingly complex properties of numbers and arithmetic, and problems demanding efficient written and mental methods of calculation. With this foundation in arithmetic, pupils are introduced to the language of algebra as a means for solving a variety of problems. Teaching in geometry and measures should consolidate and extend knowledge developed in number. Teaching should also ensure that pupils classify shapes with increasingly complex geometric properties and that they learn the vocabulary they need to describe them.

By the end of Year 6, pupils should be fluent in written methods for all four operations, including long multiplication and division, and in working with fractions, decimals and percentages.

Pupils should read, spell and pronounce mathematical vocabulary correctly.

# Year 5

| Year 5 Programme of Study (statutory requirements) | Notes and guidance (non-statutory) |
|---|---|
| **NUMBER**<br><br>**Number and place value**<br><br>Pupils should be taught to:<br><br>• read, write, order and compare numbers to at least 1,000,000 and determine the value of each digit<br><br>• count forwards or backwards in steps of powers of 10 for any given number up to 1,000,000<br><br>• interpret negative numbers in context, count forwards and backwards with positive and negative whole numbers, including through zero<br><br>• round any number up to 1,000,000 to the nearest 10, 100, 1000, 10,000 and 100,000<br><br>• solve number problems and practical problems that involve all of the above<br><br>• read Roman numerals to 1000 (M) and recognise years written in Roman numerals. | **NUMBER**<br><br>**Number and place value**<br><br>Pupils identify the place value in large whole numbers.<br><br>They continue to use number in context, including measurement. Pupils extend and apply their understanding of the number system to the decimal numbers and fractions that they have met so far.<br><br>They should recognise and describe linear number sequences, including those involving fractions and decimals, and find the term-to-term rule.<br><br>They should recognise and describe linear number sequences (for example, 3, $3\frac{1}{2}$, 4, $4\frac{1}{2}$ ...), including those involving fractions and decimals, and find the term-to-term rule in words (for example, add $\frac{1}{2}$). |
| **Number: Addition and subtraction**<br><br>Pupils should be taught to:<br><br>• add and subtract whole numbers with more than 4 digits, including using formal written methods (columnar addition and subtraction)<br><br>• add and subtract numbers mentally with increasingly large numbers<br><br>• use rounding to check answers to calculations and determine, in the context of a problem, levels of accuracy<br><br>• solve addition and subtraction multi-step problems in contexts, deciding which operations and methods to use and why. | **Addition and subtraction**<br><br>Pupils practise using the formal written methods of columnar addition and subtraction with increasingly large numbers to aid fluency (see Mathematics Appendix 1).<br><br>They practise mental calculations with increasingly large numbers to aid fluency (for example, 12,462 − 2300 = 10,162). |

# Year 5 Programme of Study (statutory requirements)

## Number: Multiplication and division

Pupils should be taught to:

- identify multiples and factors, including finding all factor pairs of a number, and common factors of two numbers.

- know and use the vocabulary of prime numbers, prime factors and composite (non-prime) numbers

- establish whether a number up to 100 is prime and recall prime numbers up to 19

- multiply numbers up to 4 digits by a one- or two-digit number using a formal written method, including long multiplication for two-digit numbers

- multiply and divide numbers mentally drawing upon known facts

- divide numbers up to 4 digits by a one-digit number using the formal written method of short division and interpret remainders appropriately for the context

- multiply and divide whole numbers and those involving decimals by 10, 100 and 1000

- recognise and use square numbers and cube numbers, and the notation for squared ($^2$) and cubed ($^3$)

- solve problems involving multiplication and division including using their knowledge of factors and multiples, squares and cubes

- solve problems involving addition, subtraction, multiplication and division and a combination of these, including understanding the meaning of the equals sign

- solve problems involving multiplication and division, including scaling by simple fractions and problems involving simple rates.

# Notes and guidance (non-statutory)

## Multiplication and division

Pupils practise and extend their use of the formal written methods of short multiplication and short division (see Mathematics Appendix 1). They apply all the multiplication tables and related division facts frequently, commit them to memory and use them confidently to make larger calculations.

They use and understand the terms factor, multiple and prime, square and cube numbers.

Pupils interpret non-integer answers to division by expressing results in different ways according to the context, including with remainders, as fractions, as decimals or by rounding (eg $98 \div 4 = {}^{98}/4 = 24 \text{ r } 2 = 24^1/_2 = 24.5 \approx 25$).

Pupils use multiplication and division as inverses to support the introduction of ratio in Year 6, for example, by multiplying and dividing by powers of 10 in scale drawings or by multiplying and dividing by powers of 1000 in converting between units such as kilometres and metres.

Distributivity can be expressed as $a(b + c) = ab + ac$.

They understand the terms factor, multiple and prime, square and cube numbers and use them to construct equivalence statements (for example, $4 \times 35 = 2 \times 2 \times 35$; $3 \times 270 = 3 \times 3 \times 9 \times 10 = 9^2 \times 10$).

Pupils use and explain the equals sign to indicate equivalence, including missing number problems (for example, $13 + 24 = 12 + 25$; $33 = 5 \times \square$).

## Year 5 Programme of Study (statutory requirements)

### Number: Fractions (including decimals and percentages)

Pupils should be taught to:

- compare and order fractions whose denominators are all multiples of the same number

- identify, name and write equivalent fractions of a given fraction, represented visually, including tenths and hundredths

- recognise mixed numbers and improper fractions and convert from one form to the other and write mathematical statements > 1 as a mixed number (for example, $2/5 + 4/5 = 6/5 = 1\,1/5$)

- add and subtract fractions with the same denominator and denominators that are multiples of the same number

- multiply proper fractions and mixed numbers by whole numbers, supported by materials and diagrams

- read and write decimal numbers as fractions (for example, 0.71 = $71/100$)

- recognise and use thousandths and relate them to tenths, hundredths and decimal equivalents

- round decimals with two decimal places to the nearest whole number and to one decimal place

- read, write, order and compare numbers with up to three decimal places

- solve problems involving numbers up to three decimal places

- recognise the per cent symbol (%) and understand that per cent relates to 'number of parts per hundred', and write percentages as a fraction with denominator 100, and as a decimal

- solve problems which require knowing percentage and decimal equivalents of $1/2$, $1/4$, $1/5$, $2/5$, $4/5$ and those fractions with a denominator of a multiple of 10 or 25.

## Notes and guidance (non-statutory)

### Fractions (including decimals and percentages)

Pupils should be taught throughout that percentages, decimals and fractions are different ways of expressing proportions.

They extend their knowledge of fractions to thousandths and connect to decimals and measures.

Pupils connect equivalent fractions > 1 to division with remainders, using the number line and other models, and hence move from these to improper and mixed fractions.

Pupils connect multiplication by a fraction to using fractions as operators (fractions of), and to division, building on work from previous years. This relates to scaling by simple fractions, including fractions > 1.

Pupils practise adding and subtracting fractions to become fluent through a variety of increasingly complex problems. They extend their understanding of adding and subtracting fractions to calculations that exceed 1 as a mixed number.

Pupils continue to practise counting forwards and backwards in simple fractions.

Pupils continue to develop their understanding of fractions as numbers, measures and operators by finding fractions of numbers and quantities.

Pupils extend counting from Year 4, using decimals and fractions including bridging zero, for example on a number line.

Pupils say, read and write decimal fractions and related tenths, hundredths and thousandths accurately and are confident in checking the reasonableness of their answers to problems.

They mentally add and subtract tenths, and one-digit whole numbers and tenths.

| Year 5 Programme of Study (statutory requirements) | Notes and guidance (non-statutory) |
|---|---|
| | They practise adding and subtracting decimals, including a mix of whole numbers and decimals, decimals with different numbers of decimal places, and complements of 1 (for example, 0.83 + 0.17 = 1). |
| | Pupils should go beyond the measurement and money models of decimals, for example by solving puzzles involving decimals. |
| | Pupils should make connections between percentages, fractions and decimals (for example, 100% represents a whole quantity and 1% is $^1/_{100}$, 50% is $^{50}/_{100}$, 25% is $^{25}/_{100}$) and relate this to finding 'fractions of'. |
| **MEASUREMENT**<br><br>Pupils should be taught to:<br><br>• convert between different units of metric measure (for example, kilometre and metre; centimetre and metre; centimetre and millimetre; gram and kilogram; litre and millilitre)<br><br>• understand and use approximate equivalences between metric units and common imperial units such as inches, pounds and pints<br><br>• measure and calculate the perimeter of composite rectilinear shapes in centimetres and metres<br><br>• calculate and compare the area of rectangles (including squares), and including using standard units, square centimetres (cm²) and square metres (m²) and estimate the area of irregular shapes<br><br>• estimate volume (for example, using 1cm³ blocks to build cuboids [including cubes]) and capacity (for example, using water)<br><br>• solve problems involving converting between units of time<br><br>• use all four operations to solve problems involving measure (for example, length, mass, volume, money) using decimal notation, including scaling. | **MEASUREMENT**<br><br>Pupils use their knowledge of place value and multiplication and division to convert between standard units.<br><br>Pupils calculate the perimeter of rectangles and related composite shapes, including using the relations of perimeter or area to find unknown lengths. Missing measures questions such as these can be expressed algebraically, for example 4 + 2b = 20 for a rectangle of sides 2cm and b cm and perimeter of 20cm.<br><br>Pupils calculate the area from scale drawings using given measurements.<br><br>Pupils use all four operations in problems involving time and money, including conversions (for example, days to weeks, expressing the answer as weeks and days). |

| Year 5 Programme of Study (statutory requirements) | Notes and guidance (non-statutory) |
|---|---|
| **GEOMETRY**<br>**Properties of shapes**<br><br>Pupils should be taught to:<br><br>• identify 3D shapes, including cubes and other cuboids, from 2D representations<br><br>• know angles are measured in degrees: estimate and compare acute, obtuse and reflex angles<br><br>• draw given angles, and measure them in degrees (°)<br><br>• identify:<br>  • angles at a point and one whole turn (total 360°)<br>  • angles at a point on a straight line and ½ a turn (total 180°)<br>  • other multiples of 90°<br><br>• use the properties of rectangles to deduce related facts and find missing lengths and angles<br><br>• distinguish between regular and irregular polygons based on reasoning about equal sides and angles.<br><br>**Geometry: Position and direction**<br><br>Pupils should be taught to:<br><br>• identify, describe and represent the position of a shape following a reflection or translation, using the appropriate language, and know that the shape has not changed.<br><br>**STATISTICS**<br><br>Pupils should be taught to:<br><br>• solve comparison, sum and difference problems using information presented in a line graph<br><br>• complete, read and interpret information in tables, including timetables. | **GEOMETRY**<br>**Properties of shapes**<br><br>Pupils become accurate in drawing lines with a ruler to the nearest millimetre, and measuring with a protractor. They use conventional markings for parallel lines and right angles.<br><br>Pupils use the term *diagonal* and make conjectures about the angles formed between sides, and between diagonals and parallel sides, and other properties of quadrilaterals, for example using dynamic geometry ICT tools.<br><br>Pupils use angle sum facts and other properties to make deductions about missing angles and relate these to missing number problems.<br><br>**Position and direction**<br><br>Pupils recognise and use reflection and translation in a variety of diagrams, including continuing to use a 2D grid and coordinates in the first quadrant. Reflection should be in lines that are parallel to the axes.<br><br>**STATISTICS**<br><br>Pupils connect their work on coordinates and scales to their interpretation of time graphs.<br><br>They begin to decide which representations of data are most appropriate and why. |

# Year 6

| Year 6 Programme of Study (statutory requirements) | Notes and guidance (non-statutory) |
|---|---|
| **NUMBER**<br><br>**Number and place value**<br><br>Pupils should be taught to:<br><br>• read, write, order and compare numbers up to 10,000,000 and determine the value of each digit<br><br>• round any whole number to a required degree of accuracy<br><br>• use negative numbers in context, and calculate intervals across zero<br><br>• solve number and practical problems that involve all of the above. | **NUMBER**<br><br>**Number and place value**<br><br>Pupils use the whole number system, including saying, reading and writing numbers accurately. |
| **Number: Addition, subtraction, multiplication and division**<br><br>Pupils should be taught to:<br><br>• multiply multi-digit numbers up to 4 digits by a two-digit whole number using the formal written method of long multiplication<br><br>• divide numbers up to 4 digits by a two-digit whole number using the formal written method of long division, and interpret remainders as whole number remainders, fractions, or by rounding, as appropriate for the context<br><br>• divide numbers up to 4 digits by a two-digit number using the formal written method of short division where appropriate, interpreting remainders according to the context<br><br>• perform mental calculations, including with mixed operations and large numbers.<br><br>• identify common factors, common multiples and prime numbers<br><br>• use their knowledge of the order of operations to carry out calculations involving the four operations<br><br>• solve addition and subtraction multi-step problems in contexts, deciding which operations and methods to use and why<br><br>• solve problems involving addition, subtraction, multiplication and division<br><br>• use estimation to check answers to calculations and determine, in the context of a problem, an appropriate degree of accuracy. | **Addition, subtraction, multiplication and division**<br><br>Pupils practise addition, subtraction, multiplication and division for larger numbers, using the formal written methods of columnar addition and subtraction, short and long multiplication, and short and long division (see Mathematics Appendix 1).<br><br>They undertake mental calculations with increasingly large numbers and more complex calculations.<br><br>Pupils continue to use all the multiplication tables to calculate mathematical statements in order to maintain their fluency.<br><br>Pupils round answers to a specified degree of accuracy, eg to the nearest 10, 20, 50 etc, but not to a specified number of significant figures.<br><br>Pupils explore the order of operations using brackets; for example, $2 + 1 \times 3 = 5$ and $(2 + 1) \times 3 = 9$.<br><br>Common factors can be related to finding equivalent fractions. |

| Year 6 Programme of Study (statutory requirements) | Notes and guidance (non-statutory) |
|---|---|
| **Number: Fractions (including decimals and percentages)**<br><br>Pupils should be taught to:<br><br>• use common factors to simplify fractions; use common multiples to express fractions in the same denomination<br><br>• compare and order fractions, including fractions >1<br><br>• add and subtract fractions with different denominators and mixed numbers, using the concept of equivalent fractions<br><br>• multiply simple pairs of proper fractions, writing the answer in its simplest form (for example, $\frac{1}{4} \times \frac{1}{2} = \frac{1}{8}$)<br><br>• divide proper fractions by whole numbers (for example, $\frac{1}{3} \div 2 = \frac{1}{6}$)<br><br>• associate a fraction with division and calculate decimal fraction equivalents (for example, 0.375) for a simple fraction (for example, $\frac{3}{8}$)<br><br>• identify the value of each digit in numbers given to three decimal places and multiply and divide numbers by 10, 100 and 1000 giving answers up to three decimal places<br><br>• multiply one-digit numbers with up to two decimal places by whole numbers<br><br>• use written division methods in cases where the answer has up to two decimal places<br><br>• solve problems which require answers to be rounded to specified degrees of accuracy<br><br>• recall and use equivalences between simple fractions, decimals and percentages, including in different contexts. | **Fractions (including decimals and percentages)**<br><br>Pupils should practise, use and understand the addition and subtraction of fractions with different denominators by identifying equivalent fractions with the same denominator. They should start with fractions where the denominator of one fraction is a multiple of the other (for example, $\frac{1}{2} + \frac{1}{8} = \frac{5}{8}$) and progress to varied and increasingly complex problems.<br><br>Pupils should use a variety of images to support their understanding of multiplication with fractions. This follows earlier work about fractions as operators (fractions of), as numbers, and as equal parts of objects, for example as parts of a rectangle.<br><br>Pupils use their understanding of the relationship between unit fractions and division to work backwards by multiplying a quantity that represents a unit fraction to find the whole quantity (for example, if $\frac{1}{4}$ of a length is 36cm, then the whole length is 36 × 4 = 144cm).<br><br>They practise calculations with simple fractions and decimal fraction equivalents to aid fluency, including listing equivalent fractions to identify fractions with common denominators.<br><br>Pupils can explore and make conjectures about converting a simple fraction to a decimal fraction (e.g. 3 ÷ 8 = 0.375). For simple fractions with recurring decimal equivalents, pupils learn about rounding the decimal to three decimal places, or other appropriate approximations depending on the context. Pupils multiply and divide numbers with up to two decimal places by one-digit and two-digit whole numbers. Pupils multiply decimals by whole numbers, starting with the simplest cases, such as 0.4 × 2 = 0.8, and in practical contexts, such as measures and money.<br><br>Pupils are introduced to the division of decimal numbers by one-digit whole numbers and, initially, in practical contexts involving measures and money. They recognise division calculations as the inverse of multiplication.<br><br>Pupils also develop their skills of rounding and estimating as a means of predicting and checking the order of magnitude of their answers to decimal calculations. This includes rounding answers to a specified degree of accuracy and checking the reasonableness of their answers. |

# Year 6 Programme of Study (statutory requirements)

## RATIO AND PROPORTION

Pupils should be taught to:

- solve problems involving the relative sizes of two quantities where missing values can be found by using integer multiplication and division facts

- solve problems involving the calculation of percentages (for example, of measures, and such as 15% of 360) and the use of percentages for comparison

- solve problems involving similar shapes where the scale factor is known or can be found

- solve problems involving unequal sharing and grouping using knowledge of fractions and multiples.

## ALGEBRA

Pupils should be taught to:

- use simple formulae
- generate and describe linear number sequences
- express missing number problems algebraically
- find pairs of numbers that satisfy an equation with two unknowns
- enumerate all possibilities of combinations of two variables.

# Notes and guidance (non-statutory)

## RATIO AND PROPORTION

Pupils recognise proportionality in contexts when the relations between quantities are in the same ratio (for example, similar shapes and recipes).

Pupils link percentages or 360° to calculating angles of pie charts.

Pupils should consolidate their understanding of ratio when comparing quantities, sizes and scale drawings by solving a variety of problems. They might use the notation $a:b$ to record their work.

Pupils solve problems involving unequal quantities eg 'for every egg you need three spoonfuls of flour', '$^3/_5$ of the class are boys'. These problems are the foundation for later formal approaches to ratio and proportion.

## ALGEBRA

Pupils should be introduced to the use of symbols and letters to represent variables and unknowns in mathematical situations that they already understand, such as:

- missing numbers, lengths, coordinates and angles
- formulae in mathematics and science
- equivalent expressions (for example, $a + b = b + a$)
- generalisations of number patterns
- number puzzles (for example, what two numbers can add up to).

# Year 6 Programme of Study (statutory requirements)

## MEASUREMENT

Pupils should be taught to:

- solve problems involving the calculation and conversion of units of measure, using decimal notation up to three decimal places where appropriate

- use, read, write and convert between standard units, converting measurements of length, mass, volume and time from a smaller unit of measure to a larger unit, and vice versa, using decimal notation to up to three decimal places

- convert between miles and kilometres

- recognise that shapes with the same areas can have different perimeters and vice versa

- recognise when it is possible to use formulae for area and volume of shapes

- calculate the area of parallelograms and triangles

- calculate, estimate and compare volume of cubes and cuboids using standard units, including cubic centimetres ($cm^3$) and cubic metres ($m^3$), and extending to other units (for example, $mm^3$ and $km^3$).

# Notes and guidance (non-statutory)

## MEASUREMENT

Pupils connect conversion (for example, from kilometres to miles) to a graphical representation as preparation for understanding linear/proportional graphs.

They know approximate conversions and are able to tell if an answer is sensible.

Using the number line, pupils use, add and subtract positive and negative integers for measures such as temperature.

They relate the area of rectangles to parallelograms and triangles, for example, by dissection, and calculate their areas, understanding and using the formulae (in words or symbols) to do this.

Pupils could be introduced to compound units for speed, such as miles per hour, and apply their knowledge in science or other subjects as appropriate.

| Year 6 Programme of Study (statutory requirements) | Notes and guidance (non-statutory) |
|---|---|
| **GEOMETRY**<br><br>**Properties of shapes**<br><br>Pupils should be taught to:<br><br>• draw 2D shapes using given dimensions and angles<br><br>• recognise, describe and build simple 3D shapes, including making nets<br><br>• compare and classify geometric shapes based on their properties and sizes and find unknown angles in any triangles, quadrilaterals, and regular polygons<br><br>• illustrate and name parts of circles, including radius, diameter and circumference and know that the diameter is twice the radius<br><br>• recognise angles where they meet at a point, are on a straight line, or are vertically opposite, and find missing angles. | **GEOMETRY**<br><br>**Properties of shapes**<br><br>Pupils draw shapes and nets accurately, using measuring tools and conventional markings and labels for lines and angles.<br><br>Pupils describe the properties of shapes and explain how unknown angles and lengths can be derived from known measurements.<br><br>These relationships might be expressed algebraically for example, $d = 2 \times r$, $a = 180 - (b + c)$. |
| **Geometry: Position and direction**<br><br>Pupils should be taught to:<br><br>• describe positions on the full coordinate grid (all four quadrants)<br><br>• draw and translate simple shapes on the coordinate plane, and reflect them in the axes. | **Position and direction**<br><br>Pupils draw and label a pair of axes in all four quadrants with equal scaling. This extends their knowledge of one quadrant to all four quadrants, including the use of negative numbers.<br><br>Pupils draw and label rectangles (including squares), parallelograms and rhombuses, specified by coordinates in the four quadrants, predicting missing coordinates using the properties of shapes. These might be expressed algebraically for example, translating vertex $(a, b)$ to $(a − 2, b + 3)$; $(a, b)$ and $(a + d, b + d)$ being opposite vertices of a square of side $d$. |
| **STATISTICS**<br><br>Pupils should be taught to:<br><br>• interpret and construct pie charts and line graphs and use these to solve problems<br><br>• calculate and interpret the mean as an average. | **STATISTICS**<br><br>Pupils connect their work on angles, fractions and percentages to the interpretation of pie charts.<br><br>Pupils both encounter and draw graphs relating two variables, arising from their own enquiry and in other subjects.<br><br>They should connect conversion from kilometres to miles in measurement to its graphical representation.<br><br>Pupils know when it is appropriate to find the mean of a data set. |

# Mathematics Appendix 1: Examples of formal written methods for addition, subtraction, multiplication and division

This appendix sets out some examples of formal written methods for all four operations to illustrate the range of methods that could be taught. It is not intended to be an exhaustive list, nor is it intended to show progression in formal written methods. For example, the exact position of intermediate calculations (superscript and subscript digits) will vary depending on the method and format used.

For multiplication, some pupils may include an addition symbol when adding partial products. For division, some pupils may include a subtraction symbol when subtracting multiples of the divisor.

## Addition and subtraction

| 789 + 642 becomes | 874 − 523 becomes | 932 − 457 becomes | 932 − 457 becomes |
|---|---|---|---|
| $$\begin{array}{r} 7\ 8\ 9 \\ +\ 6\ 4\ 2 \\ \hline 1\ 4\ 3\ 1 \\ {\scriptstyle 1\ \ 1} \end{array}$$ Answer: 1431 | $$\begin{array}{r} 8\ 7\ 4 \\ -\ 5\ 2\ 3 \\ \hline 3\ 5\ 1 \end{array}$$ Answer: 351 | $$\begin{array}{r} {}^8\!\!\not9\ {}^{12}\!\!\not3\ {}^1 2 \\ -\ 4\ 5\ 7 \\ \hline 4\ 7\ 5 \end{array}$$ Answer: 475 | $$\begin{array}{r} 9\ {}^1 3\ {}^1 2 \\ -\ \not4_5\ \not5_6\ 7 \\ \hline 4\ 7\ 5 \end{array}$$ Answer: 475 |

## Short multiplication

| 24 × 6 becomes | 342 × 7 becomes | 2741 × 6 becomes |
|---|---|---|
| $$\begin{array}{r} 2\ 4 \\ \times\ \ \ \ 6 \\ \hline 1\ 4\ 4 \\ {\scriptstyle 2} \end{array}$$ Answer: 144 | $$\begin{array}{r} 3\ 4\ 2 \\ \times\ \ \ \ \ \ 7 \\ \hline 2\ 3\ 9\ 4 \\ {\scriptstyle 2\ 1} \end{array}$$ Answer: 2394 | $$\begin{array}{r} 2\ 7\ 4\ 1 \\ \times\ \ \ \ \ \ \ \ 6 \\ \hline 1\ 6\ 4\ 4\ 6 \\ {\scriptstyle 4\ 2} \end{array}$$ Answer: 16446 |

## Long multiplication

| 24 × 16 becomes | 124 × 26 becomes | 124 × 26 becomes |
|---|---|---|
| $$\begin{array}{r} {\scriptstyle 2} \\ 2\ 4 \\ \times\ \ 1\ 6 \\ \hline 2\ 4\ 0 \\ 1\ 4\ 4 \\ \hline 3\ 8\ 4 \end{array}$$ Answer: 384 | $$\begin{array}{r} {\scriptstyle 1\ \ 2} \\ 1\ 2\ 4 \\ \times\ \ \ 2\ 6 \\ \hline 2\ 4\ 8\ 0 \\ 7\ 4\ 4 \\ \hline 3\ 2\ 2\ 4 \\ {\scriptstyle 1\ \ 1} \end{array}$$ Answer: 3224 | $$\begin{array}{r} {\scriptstyle 1\ \ 2} \\ 1\ 2\ 4 \\ \times\ \ \ 2\ 6 \\ \hline 7\ 4\ 4 \\ 2\ 4\ 8\ 0 \\ \hline 3\ 2\ 2\ 4 \\ {\scriptstyle 1\ \ 1} \end{array}$$ Answer: 3224 |

## Short division

98 ÷ 7 becomes

```
        1   4
   7 | 9 ²8
```

Answer: 14

432 ÷ 5 becomes

```
          8   6   r2
   5 | 4   3 ³2
```

Answer: 86 remainder 2

496 ÷ 11 becomes

```
          4   5   r1
  1  1 | 4   9 ⁵6
```

Answer: 45 $\frac{1}{11}$

## Long division

432 ÷ 15 becomes

```
          2   8   r12
  1  5 | 4   3   2
         3   0   0
         1   3   2
         1   2   0
             1   2
```

Answer: 28 remainder 12

432 ÷ 15 becomes

```
          2   8
  1  5 | 4   3   2
         3   0   0    15 × 20
         1   3   2
         1   2   0    15 × 8
             1   2
```

$\frac{12}{15} = \frac{4}{5}$

Answer: 28 $\frac{4}{5}$

432 ÷ 15 becomes

```
          2   8 · 8
  1  5 | 4   3   2 · 0
         3   0 ↓
         1   3   2
         1   2   0
             1   2 · 0
             1   2 · 0
                     0
```

Answer: 28.8

# Mathematics Programme of Study: Key Stage 3

## Purpose of study

Mathematics is a creative and highly inter-connected discipline that has been developed over centuries, providing the solution to some of history's most intriguing problems. It is essential to everyday life, critical to science, technology and engineering, and necessary for financial literacy and most forms of employment. A high-quality mathematics education therefore provides a foundation for understanding the world, the ability to reason mathematically, an appreciation of the beauty and power of mathematics, and a sense of enjoyment and curiosity about the subject.

## Aims

The National Curriculum for mathematics aims to ensure that all pupils:

- become **fluent** in the fundamentals of mathematics, including through varied and frequent practice with increasingly complex problems over time, so that pupils develop conceptual understanding and the ability to recall and apply knowledge rapidly and accurately

- **reason mathematically** by following a line of enquiry, conjecturing relationships and generalisations, and developing an argument, justification or proof using mathematical language

- can **solve problems** by applying their mathematics to a variety of routine and non-routine problems with increasing sophistication, including breaking down problems into a series of simpler steps and persevering in seeking solutions.

Mathematics is an interconnected subject in which pupils need to be able to move fluently between representations of mathematical ideas. The Programme of Study for Key Stage 3 is organised into apparently distinct Domains, but pupils should build on Key Stage 2 and connections across mathematical ideas to develop fluency, mathematical reasoning and competence in solving increasingly sophisticated problems. They should also apply their mathematical knowledge in science, geography, computing and other subjects.

Decisions about progression should be based on the security of pupils' understanding and their readiness to progress to the next stage. Pupils who grasp concepts rapidly should be challenged through being offered rich and sophisticated problems before any acceleration through new content in preparation for Key Stage 4. Those who are not sufficiently fluent should consolidate their understanding, including through additional practice, before moving on.

## Information and communication technology (ICT)

Calculators should not be used as a substitute for good written and mental arithmetic. In secondary schools, teachers should use their judgement about when ICT tools should be used.

## Spoken language

The National Curriculum for mathematics reflects the importance of spoken language in pupils' development across the whole curriculum – cognitively, socially and linguistically. The quality and variety of language that pupils hear and speak are key factors in developing their mathematical vocabulary and presenting a mathematical justification, argument or proof. They must be assisted in making their thinking clear to themselves as well as others and teachers should ensure that pupils build secure foundations by using discussion to probe and remedy their misconceptions.

## Attainment targets

By the end of Key Stage 3, pupils are expected to know, apply and understand the matters, skills and processes specified in the relevant Programme of Study.

**Schools are not required by law to teach the example content in grey tint or the content indicated as being non-statutory.**

# Key Stage 3

## Working mathematically

Through the mathematics content, pupils should be taught to:

**Develop fluency**

- consolidate their numerical and mathematical capability from Key Stage 2 and extend their understanding of the number system and place value to include decimals, fractions, powers and roots

- select and use appropriate calculation strategies to solve increasingly complex problems

- use algebra to generalise the structure of arithmetic, including to formulate mathematical relationships

- substitute values in expressions, rearrange and simplify expressions, and solve equations

- move freely between different numerical, algebraic, graphical and diagrammatic representations (for example, equivalent fractions, fractions and decimals, and equations and graphs)

- develop algebraic and graphical fluency, including understanding linear and simple quadratic functions

- use language and properties precisely to analyse numbers, algebraic expressions, 2D and 3D shapes, probability and statistics.

**Reason mathematically**

- extend their understanding of the number system; make connections between number relationships, and their algebraic and graphical representations

- extend and formalise their knowledge of ratio and proportion in working with measures and geometry, and in formulating proportional relations algebraically

- identify variables and express relations between variables algebraically and graphically

- make and test conjectures about patterns and relationships; look for proofs or counter-examples

- begin to reason deductively in geometry, number and algebra, including using geometrical constructions

- interpret when the structure of a numerical problem requires additive, multiplicative or proportional reasoning

- explore what can and cannot be inferred in statistical and probabilistic settings, and begin to express their arguments formally.

## Solve problems

- develop their mathematical knowledge, in part through solving problems and evaluating the outcomes, including multi-step problems

- develop their use of formal mathematical knowledge to interpret and solve problems, including in financial mathematics

- begin to model situations mathematically and express the results using a range of formal mathematical representations

- select appropriate concepts, methods and techniques to apply to unfamiliar and non-routine problems.

# Subject content

## Number

Pupils should be taught to:

- understand and use place value for decimals, measures and integers of any size

- order positive and negative integers, decimals and fractions; use the number line as a model for ordering of the real numbers; use the symbols =, ≠, <, >, ≤, ≥

- use the concepts and vocabulary of prime numbers, factors (or divisors), multiples, common factors, common multiples, highest common factor, lowest common multiple, prime factorisation, including using product notation and the unique factorisation property

- use the four operations, including formal written methods, applied to integers, decimals, proper and improper fractions, and mixed numbers, all both positive and negative

- use conventional notation for the priority of operations, including brackets, powers, roots and reciprocals

- recognise and use relationships between operations including inverse operations

- use integer powers and associated real roots (square, cube and higher), recognise powers of 2, 3, 4, 5 and distinguish between exact representations of roots and their decimal approximations

- interpret and compare numbers in standard form $A \times 10^n$ $1 \le A < 10$, where n is a positive or negative integer or zero

- work interchangeably with terminating decimals and their corresponding fractions (such as 3.5 and $^7/_2$ or 0.375 and $^3/_8$)

- define percentage as 'number of parts per hundred', interpret percentages and percentage changes as a fraction or a decimal, interpret these multiplicatively, express one quantity as a percentage of another, compare two quantities using percentages, and work with percentages greater than 100%

- interpret fractions and percentages as operators

- use standard units of mass, length, time, money and other measures, including with decimal quantities

- round numbers and measures to an appropriate degree of accuracy (for example, to a number of decimal places or significant figures)

- use approximation through rounding to estimate answers and calculate possible resulting errors expressed using inequality notation $a < x \le b$

- use a calculator and other technologies to calculate results accurately and then interpret them appropriately

- appreciate the infinite nature of the sets of integers, real and rational numbers.

## Algebra

Pupils should be taught to:

- use and interpret algebraic notation, including:
  - $ab$ in place of $a \times b$
  - $3y$ in place of $y + y + y$ and $3 \times y$

- $a^2$ in place of $a \times a$, $a^3$ in place of $a \times a \times a$; $a^2b$ in place of $a \times a \times b$
- $a/b$ in place of $a \div b$
- coefficients written as fractions rather than as decimals
- brackets

- substitute numerical values into formulae and expressions, including scientific formulae
- understand and use the concepts and vocabulary of expressions, equations, inequalities, terms and factors
- simplify and manipulate algebraic expressions to maintain equivalence by:
  - collecting like terms
  - multiplying a single term over a bracket
  - taking out common factors
  - expanding products of two or more binomials
- understand and use standard mathematical formulae; rearrange formulae to change the subject
- model situations or procedures by translating them into algebraic expressions or formulae and by using graphs
- use algebraic methods to solve linear equations in one variable (including all forms that require rearrangement)
- work with coordinates in all four quadrants
- recognise, sketch and produce graphs of linear and quadratic functions of one variable with appropriate scaling, using equations in $x$ and $y$ and the Cartesian plane
- interpret mathematical relationships both algebraically and graphically
- reduce a given linear equation in two variables to the standard form $y = mx + c$; calculate and interpret gradients and intercepts of graphs of such linear equations numerically, graphically and algebraically
- use linear and quadratic graphs to estimate values of $y$ for given values of $x$ and vice versa and to find approximate solutions of simultaneous linear equations
- find approximate solutions to contextual problems from given graphs of a variety of functions, including piece-wise linear, exponential and reciprocal graphs
- generate terms of a sequence from either a term-to-term or a position-to-term rule
- recognise arithmetic sequences and find the $n$th term
- recognise geometric sequences and appreciate other sequences that arise.

## Ratio, proportion and rates of change

Pupils should be taught to:

- change freely between related standard units (for example time, length, area, volume/capacity, mass)
- use scale factors, scale diagrams and maps
- express one quantity as a fraction of another, where the fraction is less than 1 and greater than 1
- use ratio notation, including reduction to simplest form

- divide a given quantity into two parts in a given part:part or part:whole ratio; express the division of a quantity into two parts as a ratio
- understand that a multiplicative relationship between two quantities can be expressed as a ratio or a fraction
- relate the language of ratios and the associated calculations to the arithmetic of fractions and to linear functions
- solve problems involving percentage change, including: percentage increase, decrease and original value problems and simple interest in financial mathematics
- solve problems involving direct and inverse proportion, including graphical and algebraic representations
- use compound units such as speed, unit pricing and density to solve problems.

## Geometry and measures

Pupils should be taught to:

- derive and apply formulae to calculate and solve problems involving: perimeter and area of triangles, parallelograms, trapezia, volume of cuboids (including cubes) and other prisms (including cylinders)
- calculate and solve problems involving: perimeters of 2D shapes (including circles), areas of circles and composite shapes
- draw and measure line segments and angles in geometric figures, including interpreting scale drawings
- derive and use the standard ruler and compass constructions (perpendicular bisector of a line segment, constructing a perpendicular to a given line from/at a given point, bisecting a given angle); recognise and use the perpendicular distance from a point to a line as the shortest distance to the line
- describe, sketch and draw using conventional terms and notations: points, lines, parallel lines, perpendicular lines, right angles, regular polygons, and other polygons that are reflectively and rotationally symmetric
- use the standard conventions for labelling the sides and angles of triangle ABC, and know and use the criteria for congruence of triangles
- derive and illustrate properties of triangles, quadrilaterals, circles, and other plane figures (for example, equal lengths and angles) using appropriate language and technologies
- identify properties of, and describe the results of, translations, rotations and reflections applied to given figures
- identify and construct congruent triangles, and construct similar shapes by enlargement, with and without coordinate grids
- apply the properties of angles at a point, angles at a point on a straight line, vertically opposite angles
- understand and use the relationship between parallel lines and alternate and corresponding angles
- derive and use the sum of angles in a triangle and use it to deduce the angle sum in any polygon, and to derive properties of regular polygons
- apply angle facts, triangle congruence, similarity and properties of quadrilaterals to derive results about angles and sides, including

**⊞SCHOLASTIC**

Pythagoras' Theorem, and use known results to obtain simple proofs

- use Pythagoras' Theorem and trigonometric ratios in similar triangles to solve problems involving right-angled triangles
- use the properties of faces, surfaces, edges and vertices of cubes, cuboids, prisms, cylinders, pyramids, cones and spheres to solve problems in 3D
- interpret mathematical relationships both algebraically and geometrically.

## Probability

Pupils should be taught to:

- record, describe and analyse the frequency of outcomes of simple probability experiments involving randomness, fairness, equally and unequally likely outcomes, using appropriate language and the 0–1 probability scale
- understand that the probabilities of all possible outcomes sum to 1
- enumerate sets and unions/intersections of sets systematically, using tables, grids and Venn diagrams
- generate theoretical sample spaces for single and combined events with equally likely, mutually exclusive outcomes and use these to calculate theoretical probabilities.

## Statistics

Pupils should be taught to:

- describe, interpret and compare observed distributions of a single variable through: appropriate graphical representation involving discrete, continuous and grouped data; and appropriate measures of central tendency (mean, mode, median) and spread (range, consideration of outliers)
- construct and interpret appropriate tables, charts, and diagrams, including frequency tables, bar charts, pie charts, and pictograms for categorical data, and vertical line (or bar) charts for ungrouped and grouped numerical data
- describe simple mathematical relationships between two variables (bivariate data) in observational and experimental contexts and illustrate using scatter graphs.

# Notes

**Babcock** ldp
partners in education

# Primary English & Mathematics

The Babcock LDP Primary English Adviser team work with schools and other organisations through:

- Sharing resources and ideas via a popular website **www.babcock-education.co.uk/ldp/literacy**. The site offers a wealth of free resources and support as well as signposts to publications which are practical ideas for the classroom.
- High quality training in all aspects of Primary English. Training can be centrally arranged or bespoke for individual schools or clusters of schools.
- Working alongside school improvement colleagues to support schools pre and post Ofsted including audit and action planning support.

Key areas supported by the team include:
- Planning for the New National Curriculum
- Grammar, Spelling and Phonics
- Talk for Writing
- Developing the teaching of reading: guided reading, Reciprocal Reading, reading for pleasure and researched reading interventions.

To find out more about the work of the team, visit our website and sign up for our newsletter, or contact: **rebecca.cosgrave@babcockinternational.com** **www.babcock-education.co.uk/ldp/literacy**

The Babcock LDP Primary Maths Adviser team work with schools and their partners to support the development of mathematics across the primary years.

All our work is underpinned by research and is based on the belief that thinking is at the heart of mathematics and therefore at the heart of mathematics teaching and learning.

The maths team holds the National Centre for Excellence in Teaching of Mathematics – National CPD Standard and are NCETM Professional Development Accredited Leads.

To find out more about the work of the team, visit our website and sign up for our newsletter, or contact: **ruth.trundley@babcockinternational.com** **www.babcock-education.co.uk/ldp/maths**

66 This project has had a fantastic impact upon all learners who have received the intervention. 99 (Assistant headteacher, West Croft)

66 Thank you again for today – I know that the staff will have really appreciated seeing an actual guided group being taught 'live' and admired your bravery as well as the skills that you demonstrated. 99 (Primary School headteacher, Bickleigh Down)

# Working in partnership for better outcomes